From Beer to Maternity

From Beer to Maternity

Maggie Lamond Simone

BRODMAN PUBLISHING
Baldwinsville, New York

Published by:
BRODMAN PUBLISHING
Baldwinsville, NY
1-315-635-2339

From Beer to Maternity
by Maggie Lamond Simone

All columns were originally published in the Syracuse, New York Herald American (1995-2001) and Family Times: The Parenting Guide of Central New York (2002-2009).

Publisher's Cataloging-in-Publication
(Provided by Quality Books, Inc.)

Simone, Maggie Lamond.
    From beer to maternity / Maggie Lamond Simone.
    p. cm.
    Essays.
    LCCN 2009926466
    ISBN-13: 978-0-615-28992-2
    ISBN-10: 0-615-28992-4

    1. Simone, Maggie Lamond. 2. Women journalists— United States—Biography. 3. Life change events—Biography. 4. Life change events—Humor. 5. Women—Biography. I. Title.

PN4874.S514A3 2009   070'.92
                                            QBI09-600090

Content edit by Tina Schwab Grenis

Book and cover design by Peri Poloni-Gabriel, Knockout Design, www.knockoutbooks.com

Printed in the United States of America

Contents

Prologue

O N A BEAUTIFUL FRIDAY EVENING 20 years ago, I left
a downtown happy hour and headed for my favorite
neighborhood bar. After a few miles on the highway, I couldn't
help noticing that I'd plowed head-on into a construction bar-
rier. Unhurt and undaunted, and peering through the thin strip
of windshield visible underneath the hood which had popped
up in the collision and now blocked my view, I pulled into
the breakdown lane of the highway and continued on my way
to the bar. I'd almost made it when the flashing red-and-blue
lights appeared in my rearview mirror. I was too hammered to
realize I might be in trouble.

I pulled over and an officer approached the car, flashlight in
hand. After looking over the completely totaled front end, he
shined the light into the driver's window and said, "What the
hell are you doing?"

Thinking he was being merely conversational, I replied,
"I'm heading to Shifty's!"

He took a deep breath and said, "OK. Step out of the car, please."

I did as I was told, and he put me in the back seat of the police cruiser. He put up some flares, called a tow truck, and finally sat in the front seat to wait with me. After a few moments he said, "I'm not going to ticket you. You look like a nice girl who just made a very big mistake, and I want you to think long and hard about what you've done. Your car is totaled. You could have killed someone or been killed yourself. I'm giving you a chance to get your life together, and I suggest you take it."

I listened to his firm words and nodded in agreement. Then I asked if I could play with the Breathalyzer, since he wasn't going to be using it anyway. After the tow truck arrived and dragged my little tin can of a car to the car graveyard, the officer started to drive me home. And I said, "Hey, Shifty's is right around the corner. Can you just drop me there, you know, since I won't be driving or anything?"

He shook his head in complete disbelief, pulled up in front of the bar, and let me out.

The next morning, when I realized what had transpired, I went to my first AA meeting, and have not had a drink since.

I was almost 30, and I was pretty sure that life as I knew it was over. No more alcohol meant no more fun. No more bars. No more parties. No more being drunk, which I was sure made me more attractive, wittier, and a much better dancer. But it didn't matter. I had to quit, so I did.

Of course, it wasn't as easy as that; there were months and months of misery, self-pity and the usual fear accompanied by any life-altering event. But slowly, I started coming up for air and realized the world was still going on. It hadn't stopped. And then I had the darnedest realization.

Not only had the world not stopped, it hadn't stopped being funny. Turns out it wasn't just the booze all those years; people and life simply amuse me. On the flip side, but of equal import, came the almost insulting awareness that I could still do stupid things; that wasn't just the booze either. And sobriety provided the added benefit of ensuring that I clearly remembered those stupid things for the rest of my life.

With the dawn of this new era came a renewed sense of purpose. I had a decade's worth of life to catch up on. I went to graduate school, earned a black belt in karate, started dating men with whom "future" did not involve holidays spent at the local pub. It wasn't always easy, but it was usually a learning experience.

After those first couple years of life sans hangovers, I also realized it was time to start writing in earnest. After finishing my master's degree in journalism, I promptly began pestering Charlie, an editor at the Syracuse, NY daily paper, for a column. For two years I wheedled, begged, negotiated, accepted defeat, then came back arguing for my cause. It was almost like the stages of grief...which was, I'm sure, what I was giving Charlie all that time.

But they needed me. At the time our paper had a black woman's column, a single man's column, and a married mother's column. They did not have *my* perspective, a single white woman on the verge — of growing up, dating, marriage, kids, and just plain life. It was as though I was being born at 30, looking at the world through newly sober, yet oldly cynical eyes. I was the Mary Tyler Moore of the nineties, except that I smashed a few cars and lost a few years before happily and naively tossing my beret in the air.

Somewhere in those two years I also managed to sell a column to *Cosmopolitan* magazine. When it finally came out in print, I walked into the newspaper, showed it to Charlie, and said, "There. See? I don't suck." Within a month I had my column. It began in 1995 as a weekly column in the Sunday paper, and six years later it went with me to a monthly parenting magazine because, as many people will attest, being funny all the time with two young children is not always easy. Or possible.

In the 15 years since its inception, the column has documented my days of being single and alone for the first time, re-entering the dating world as a sober person, dating, getting engaged, getting married, getting pregnant, having kids, and finding my life again after all of that. Sometimes it's funny, sometimes not. Sometimes the not-so-funny things are important, too.

What it is, though, is honest. My column has allowed me to show people — at whatever stage they're at in life — that they don't have to be perfect to be OK. There are no books on "What to Expect When Your Boyfriend Leaves You for His High School Crush," or "What to Expect When Your Child Takes a Year to Potty Train." But that doesn't mean people don't need to know that this stuff happens.

And more important, that they can survive when it does. Sometimes even laughing.

—m—

The Fog Lifts to Reveal...
A New Type of Fog

THERE IS NO SHAME in living alone. It is a time of self-discovery, of Getting to Know Oneself. It is, however, just a bit embarrassing to live alone for the first time in 30 years, possessing absolutely no knowledge of how to care for myself. None. Nada. Zip. I can dress myself, work the VCR and start my car. And aren't those really the basics?

As a recent quitter of all things alcohol, as well as a newly minted graduate school survivor, I have felt the need to strike out on my own, and break the proverbial apron strings of my girlfriends/boyfriends/adoptive families, etc. I'm ready. Heck, I'm 30. I really need to be ready. Unfortunately, what I've discovered is that what I learned in school emphatically does not apply to real life. I believe the dead giveaway may have been the tears in the grocery store because there are no directions on a can of French-cut beans.

It seems, then, that there are certain points I should have been picking up on these last few decades that warranted a tad more than passing notice. As queen of the clueless, I would have traded my mother to learn these things from a book. Since I didn't, the philanthropist in me has decided to share my revelations in the hope of sparing even one person the grief.

The most important realization to date is that education and real life are about as related as point sparring and street fighting — just because you're good at one doesn't mean you're not going to get your butt kicked in the other.

The most immediate solo challenge — at any age — is money management. We must adopt a budget which should include food, shelter, furnishings, student loans, car payment, insurance, clothes, parking, a little tiny social life, and, of course, student loans, to which great attention should be paid. Apparently, defaulting on one's loans can lead to credit problems for approximately the rest of one's life...or so I hear.

The other very important financial lesson is that money withdrawn from an ATM is not, in fact, money from God. The sooner you accept this, the better.

Physically taking care of ourselves is another lesson we should learn really fast. Sadly, many of us have been, as opposed to roommates, more like pets who pay rent; we unconditionally love anyone who feeds us. Learning to cook and clean at this late date becomes an exercise in futility. Does tin foil count as metal in a microwave? Is there some kind of statute of limitations on food, and if so, is it written down somewhere? Egg cartons, for example, often display a month and day of expiration, but no year. This does not help me.

Cleaning will also be high on my list of Things to Teach My Children. I can handle the basics (picking up large clumps of dirt, for instance), but as I and my whisk broom wander uncomprehendingly from room to room, I admit sheer, unadulterated terror at the prospect of mopping my floors or figuring out the dishwasher. I honestly don't remember ever having to do these things. And what about washing curtains? How do you get them down? And won't those hooks damage the lingerie?

My bathroom has become my nemesis, a viable enemy and daily challenge. Aside from the obvious philosophical questions (if I live alone, why do I close the door?), it has unlocked fears far beyond Hitchcock. I could face Norm's dagger with much more bravado than when, say, whipping back the shower curtain and facing a spider the size of my left shoe. For you Twilight Zone buffs, by the way, the spider does not come back bigger if you flush it down the drain. Although I do keep looking.

Which leads to yet another janitorial black hole and general nuisance in my newfound existence: clogged pipes. In my previous life, the one where people did this for me, all I had to say was, "The sink is clogged. Somebody fix the sink." Now, alone and proud, I reach for the omnipotent Heavy Duty Drano, "for those stubborn clogs, like hair and spiders." Incidentally, that warning label is not merely conversational. It really does burn your skin.

Living alone does have its advantages. For instance, I am rarely sick anymore — without the sympathy, why bother? But in general, learning 30 years worth of details overnight has been a bit overwhelming. What exactly is a "Phillips-head screwdriver," and why do furniture people assume I own one?

When hanging a painting, it is apparently helpful to learn the dictionary definition of "stud." When things get dirty, you can't just throw them out. Simple logic, which I have been systematically dodging since birth.

I will concede that if school taught me all I needed to know about life, I'd have probably stopped growing a long time ago. And if I didn't learn these things the hard way I'd probably never learn them at all. But I would be remiss if I didn't admit that while I would no longer trade my mother, I would definitely dip into my 401K for a Dr. Spock guide for grown-ups.

Because frankly, if everything I know I learned in kindergarten, then I must have missed a day.

—⁓—

THE LATEST STATISTICS ARE OUT: We as a society are waiting longer to get married; divorce is on a slow but steady decline; the number of two-parent families is on the rise; life expectancy is gradually increasing. But what, you may ask, does it all mean?

Well, I'll tell you what it means. It means I've been right all along. I am perfectly on track to be growing up at 30. It is OK to still be single. Heck, it's becoming the style.

Here's my theory. If old people are living longer, then young people are staying kids longer. All this time I thought it was just a flimsy and not altogether viable excuse for my behavior and lifestyle, but it turns out to be true. Back in the old days, when the average age of death was 60, you were an adult at 18 or 20. You had to be; your life was one-third over.

Now, however, tons of people are living to be 100. True story. I read the obituaries every day (no, not for ex-boyfriends

— how petty do you think I am?) and almost all of the people in them are really old. Younger people, then, are younger longer.

Look at it this way. Assume you're going to live to 100. At 20, then, you're only one-fifth through your life, which back in the old days would figure out to be about 12, right? You certainly can't expect a 12-year-old to fall in love and get married and not go through any severe growing pains that could lead to divorce. Heck, they still have puberty to get through.

Both parties would eventually grow up, and they may look at each other one day and say, "You know, honey, I guess I thought you'd end up with bigger breasts," or "Sorry, baby, but I didn't realize your voice was never going to change." And the marriage would end. They've dissolved over less.

I think that's what happened to us these last couple decades. Science has allowed us to live longer, but we didn't do the adjustment on the other end. Well, I did, but everyone mocked me for it. One of the major considerations in my life choices has been that I haven't felt grown up enough to take some of these serious steps like marriage and children, and what do you know? I wasn't.

People in their late teens and 20s today are not what they were in the 1950s and 1960s. Today they're still kids. Back then they were middle-aged. And I mean that in the nicest possible way.

Fortunately, it appears that people are catching on now, which I think explains the decreasing divorce rate. The longer you wait to get married, the better chance you have of meeting up with someone who has already grown up and can be relatively relied upon to not undergo any 180-degree personality changes.

You can get married and know that in 10 years your partner probably won't have changed to the point where you can no longer tolerate him (assuming you could tolerate him in the beginning and were not blinded by his wealth or cute butt). So you can have kids and buy a house, safe in the belief that you've got a darn good shot at being together in 50 years. At least, that's the way I look at it.

And the other advantage to marrying late is that it eliminates the pesky fidelity issue. The older they are when you snag 'em, the less anybody else will want 'em; am I right?

So yes, everyone else is finally catching up to my way of thinking. If we're going to be living longer, we may as well get married later and give ourselves a decent chance at marital longevity. And of course, marrying later helps ease the commitment problem that seems to permeate today's society, because "'til death do we part" clause isn't as frightening at 35 as it would have been at 20. I mean, come on. I could see being with the same guy for 40 or 50 years, but 70?

No way. Might cramp my style.

—⚒—

I ALWAYS CONSIDERED MYSELF a simple person with simple needs. Low-maintenance, don't like a lot of moving parts, shy away from technology, sleep with a teddy bear. A 1990s kind of girl with 1950s kind of values. I used to think this, until last night.

Last night I dreamed I tried to make coffee and my state-of-the-art, two-minute coffee maker didn't work. I panicked, because I can barely spell "percolator" let alone operate one, and I need coffee in the morning like most people need air. But then I remembered the instant.

Relieved, I stuck a cup of water in the microwave, and it didn't work. Jeez, I thought. If the boyfriend thought I was edgy, he could've found a better way to tell me. But no problem; I can handle this. You just put some water into a kettle… wait, I don't own a kettle. Nobody owns a kettle. OK, you just put some water into a pan and turn on the stove…if you know how to turn on your stove, which I don't.

Wanting some answers, I paged my boyfriend, only to be greeted with a high-pitched squeal bordering on dog-only tone quality. I then opted for his cell phone, safe in the knowledge that while he doesn't actually shower with it, it sits and waits for him on the sink. Upon dialing, however, I got nothing but dead air. Real dead air this time.

I was growing impatient. I showered and was getting ready to face my unseen enemy, when I discovered to my further dismay that the blowdryer had joined the forces of evil. This may not be traumatic for the general public, but the general public has never seen Ronald McDonald with his clown-foot caught in a light socket.

In a quandary but still in dire need of coffee, I stuffed my hair into a cap and headed to the bank because naturally I would have no cash when I actually needed some, but no problem. The ATM machine and I are tight. What else in life actually gives you money for pushing its buttons?

So I got to the bank, and guess what? No ATM! I had to go INTO the bank to get money. I pondered this concept momentarily, acknowledged that I had no clue how it was done, and just barged in. I approached the person behind the counter ("teller," I believe he's called) and looked at him blankly for what seemed like hours until forming the words, "I need cash."

From the fear on his face and the way his hand shot underneath the counter, it was evident that I could have said it better. So I quickly added, "I have an account here. I forgot how to withdraw." In his relief that I wasn't in fact robbing him, he was more than happy to fill out the required slip and send me away.

I bought my coffee and headed home, hoping to put Hell Morning behind me. I settled in at the computer to write to my mom about it, but lo and behold, it too would not work. Apparently it was napping, a much more palatable explanation than believing it just wanted to see me try to write with a pen. Which it knew I couldn't do. And which I probably could no longer even hold without visual instructions.

Defeated, I plopped down on my couch, which doesn't have any mechanical parts that can fail, and reached for the trusty remote, which does. This was apparently the last straw, because I woke up in a cold sweat clutching my teddy bear like it was the last thing on earth.

When I recovered and had my coffee, I came to the undeniable conclusion that I'm not exactly what I thought. I am, instead, a 1990s woman with 1990s values. But I'm also still a simple person with simple needs because, when it comes to making life easier, it's really very easy.

I want it all, and I want it now.

—⁓—

MY INTERCOM BEEPED AT WORK the other day, and this nice young woman on the other end asked me if I would write a recommendation for her for graduate school. It was one of the more disorienting experiences of my recent past. This is a very adult task, requested of one who still sleeps with a teddy bear.

With as much cool as I could muster after being clubbed with a verbal 2x4, I asked her if she had the right extension; didn't she want someone older, with more experience, more time in the trenches? "Well, yes," she stammered. "That's why I'm asking you."

As mature as she would suggest it is, my mind could not comprehend her reasoning. I'm only 33 — too young to recommend a restaurant, let alone a fellow writer. When I was looking for recommendations for school, I turned to much more respected and, most important, older people. Without my knowledge and certainly without my consent, I apparently have become just such an older person.

And it has forced the realization that I am no longer tucked in at night.

There is a part of me that has inherently assumed that I am simply not an adult yet, possibly because I am still short. With four brothers more than 6 feet tall, I think I have been waiting for that last growth spurt to blast me into adulthood. Absent such a spurt, I must still be stuck somewhere between adolescence and The Final Frontier — a location that was just fine with me, thanks. People feed me, and I get to stay up late. Can't beat it.

This young woman's request consequently led me to ponder what could well be my first thought as an acknowledged grownup: How does one know when the line has been crossed? What are the criteria, the guidelines for maturity, for actually feeling like an adult? I know many kids who are more responsible than me, and many adults who aren't. So how do we know?

Retrospectively, I now see that there were a series of warning signs, clues that I was subtly being catapulted out of the womb of youth. If only I had recognized them, maybe this tragedy could have been prevented. Instead, I will hold my head high and write this girl's recommendation, and issue this warning to those who still have a chance to run. You know you're growing up when:

- ∽ You change the oil in your car before the engine blows up. This involves periodically reading the little sticker in the top corner of your windshield and actually taking note when the date on it has passed.

- ∽ You get a real cart in the grocery store instead of grabbing that little basket that holds 12 things and leaving when it's full, whether you're done shopping or not.

- ∽ Your arm flails across the passenger seat when you slam on the brakes, effectively preventing your briefcase and phone from blasting through the windshield — because hey, someday it might be a kid there.

- ∽ You buy a dozen Mother's and Father's Day cards, and they're all for your friends.

- ∽ You hire a neighborhood kid to cut the grass because darn it, there just aren't enough hours in the day.

- ∽ You find yourself dusting and vacuuming when no one is coming over.

- ∽ You eat your Chinese takeout off of real dishes.

 ∞ You go to Florida with SPF 30 sunscreen, and use it.

 ∞ You pass baby clothes in the mall and think, "How adorable!" instead of, "Eek! Who's that small?"

 ∞ You stop scanning the obituaries for ex-lovers because it's just no fun anymore.

 ∞ You find yourself singing to the Muzak in the elevator. Out loud.

And there you have it. There is no holiday to mark it, no cards, no presents. You just wake up one day and someone asks you to write a recommendation. You realize that somewhere along the line, willingly or not, you grew up, inheriting all of the responsibility that comes with it. Whatever conspiracy of events collaborated to do the deed, the deed is done. And when you curl up in bed that first night, you can't help but notice something else.

Even your teddy bear looks proud.

—m—

UNFORTUNATELY, STATISTICAL EXPERIENCE SHOWS that one in two marriages end in divorce. My own experience shows that one in two relationships end, period. That means there are an awful lot of people out there getting sweaty palms just thinking about asking someone out for what could be the first time in a decade or two. So here's a little tip for those unclear on the concept of DOA — dating once again: it's not like the first time around. We're grown-ups now. No more passing notes in study hall.

Here we are, in the prime of our lives, with financial security, careers, homes, hobbies and routines, jettisoned back into a world most of us left behind — gladly — many years ago. And if that isn't difficult enough, we're dating people who've gone through similar scripts, with generally similar attitudes. If dating is "courting," then a date must be a court and we are all OJ.

Remember the good old days of middle school, when you could call someone your "boyfriend" without busting out in giggles at the sound of it? Going steady meant sitting at the same lunch table. Being involved meant walking together, and notes were the communication method of choice. Eye contact would leave me breathless for a week. I spent my entire adolescence writing, staring, and hyperventilating.

Dating is much more complicated this time. We all want to be loved, but few of us are inclined anymore to rearrange our schedules for it, let alone give up our independence. By this age, most of us single folk are pretty content with our self-centeredness, and in fact consider it a lifestyle, if not an art form.

Another major obstacle to dating as post-college, pre-dead individuals is the obvious — where do we find the date? Sounds simple, doesn't it? Just watch TV and you'll see that we should be finding love in high-class bars ordering Michelob Ultras with our extremely hip and stylish friends, or possibly white-water rafting with a similarly trendy group, wearing very causal yet tasteful clothes and drinking Molson Golden.

Well, I've got a news flash for you, folks: Life ain't like the commercials. I work 50 hours a week and take karate and run another 10 hours a week and have parents and friends and nieces and nephews and favorite television shows and about the last thing I feel like doing at night is getting dressed and going out. And I'm just not meeting a lot of men in my living room.

So why can't I find a date in the places I spend time? News flash No. 2: Dating co-workers is taboo. Dating bosses is taboo. Dating subordinates is taboo. Dating clients is taboo. Working out makes me sweat, and I'm just not feeling my sexiest with that "Excuse me, are you having a stroke?" look. And the bar scene? Eh. My friends can't always get sitters, and I not only don't get proofed anymore; they actually chuckle and wave me in, like I'm going in to look for my daughter or something. It hurts, I tell you.

No thanks. There must be other ways. A policeman friend wanted to meet my neighbor, so I told him to pull her over. Apparently she was not amused. Blind dates and personal ads are nice, but they'd be nicer with resumes, photos and references. And obviously one does not want to appear desperate, being branded with the dreaded DWI (dating with intent) and risk never again having contact with the opposite sex.

There is just nothing easy about dating once again. Everyone's on the defensive, too shy or afraid to get involved or unfamiliar with procedure. But someday you may find someone you like who doesn't work with you and doesn't work out with you and maybe you just saw him in the grocery store and like the way he looked — so what do you do? What exactly is protocol anymore? How do you get a date? How do you close the deal?

Relax. You just let me know. I'll try to slide him a note.

—·∞·—

THERE WAS A STORY RECENTLY about a couple with a 16-page prenuptial agreement, setting forth such details as who'll do the laundry and how often they'll have sex, and I thought, wow. I have trouble just meeting men. How will I find one to marry if I have to write down all of the rules? (Of *course* I date men who can read. That's not what I meant.)

I thought prenuptials were intended to ease a split. In fact, I told my boyfriend that if we got divorced (which would mean we'd have to get married, wouldn't it, honey?) I'd happily give him half of everything I own. He replied, "Gee, that's awfully nice of you, but I think half of nothing is pretty much...um... nothing." Hey, buster, it's the thought that counts.

Anyway, this new concept seems instead to define the ground rules for marriage, a process I typically refer to as "dating." But that's OK, because it eliminates that tiresome courting phase, the last bastion of the true commitment-phobe. Now you can meet someone, hand him the rules and marry him. If he breaks the rules, turn to the divorce section and carry on.

In keeping with the 1990s, then, I conferred with fellow graduates of the "If They Can Put a Man on the Moon, Why Not Put 'em All There?" support group. We pooled our collective past lives and compiled a list of potential requirements for a happy marriage. To simplify things, "we" means the ones who've dated the idiots, and "you" means the ones we haven't dated yet. The guys, that is; not the idiots. Necessarily.

The foremost rule is that both parties must agree to the definition of "monogamy." Being married to one person at a time means only having sex with that one person. Period. Not one person at a time.

Speaking of sex, we're for it. Daily, weekly; doesn't matter. We won't set rules about frequency, but we will insist that it be with our husbands. This means that you must come home at night.

We'll share household tasks. For example, if we cook, you do the dishes. This involves slightly more effort than bringing your plate into the kitchen. And "cooking," for the record, doesn't include ordering pizza on your nights.

If we find jewelry in our beds that isn't ours, don't pretend it was supposed to be a surprise for us. Be honest. We'll still leave you, but we'll disrespect you less.

No getting drunk for other than special occasions. The fact that it's Tuesday is not inherently cause for celebration.

You can leave the toilet seat up if you'll clean the bathroom. That, my friends, is only fair.

We'll share responsibility for the dog, which doesn't mean you play with him and we clean up his poop. Corollary: No using the dog to pick up women.

We sometimes have bad PMS weeks (no, smart alec, there are no good ones; some are just worse than others.) When this happens, don't condescend to us, don't pity us, and don't try the "sympathy period" ploy. Just get out of our way.

Don't take us for granted. The fact that we've chosen to be with you should increase our worth, not eliminate it.

Don't criticize, embarrass or yell at us in public. Actually, don't do it in private, either.

Call if you're going to be late. Tip: If you're late because you're at another woman's home, you may want to ask her to be quiet before you dial.

Don't refer to us as your "ball and chain." Unless you're curious about what that might really feel like.

Lastly, you can look at other women; you can even occasionally commit the classic "adultery in your heart." If, however, it spreads to other parts of your body, take a walk. And keep going.

This is just a partial list reflecting some relationship behaviors we've tried before and didn't particularly like. Our agreement doesn't demand perfection, and we don't think we're asking too much. So there you have it, gentlemen.

Line forms to the left.

—⁓—

IN ONE OF MY FAVORITE MOVIES, a young gay man delivering the eulogy for his partner said that the partner had always preferred funerals to weddings; it was easier to get enthusiastic about a ceremony he had an outside chance of being involved in.

While my circumstances may be different, I'm beginning to see what he means.

This year's wedding season, thankfully on the wane, has found me reading the wedding announcements like my parents read the obituaries, and with essentially the same response when spotting a friend: "(Sigh.) Another one bites the dust."

I mean that in the best possible way, of course. But the older I get, the more I realize that weddings are more than just a really big cake and the chicken dance.

One of the revelations of this particular wedding season is the somewhat mind-boggling expense involved in attending them. One or two may be manageable, but I'm in my 30s. My friends are dropping like flies. I've spent more time at the mall this summer than I did in my entire adolescence, and prices have gone up. New dresses, new shoes, new accessories — now I know why people cry at weddings. And it's not happiness, as previously thought.

It has also not escaped me that many of those getting married are on Round Two, as it were. I vaguely recall buying toasters for many of these marriages several years ago, most of which probably still work (the appliances, obviously). I now find myself in the irritating position of buying more appliances for people who already have at least one and maybe two of every possible thing, while I myself still have nothing.

I frankly don't think it's fair that I can't get presents just because I don't get married. The fact that I'm single does not mean I don't need a blender. Between the engagement party, bridal shower, bachelor party and wedding, for an average of four friends per season, a person could go broke furnishing other people's homes, sometimes twice.

And while I have toyed with the idea of marriage for the booty value, I can't quite bring myself to do it. I'm just not that cold. I think, therefore, that in all fairness I should receive presents for saying "no" to the guys who have asked me to marry them. Now *that* took some guts and deserves gifts.

Bringing an escort can also be a source of irritation at this point in life, depending on how well you know your date. If involved in a relationship in which the "m" word is still taboo, for example, be very careful. I have found it helpful to not get too misty or allow any type of longing to cross one's face, for fear that one's date may actually bolt. I have also found it helpful to have pre-printed cards handy, reading something like,

"The fact that I enjoy weddings doesn't mean I want to marry you. I enjoy the opera, too. Doesn't mean I sing."

Maybe I'm jealous. I'm willing to admit the possibility that I am simply envious of people who have found love and happiness when it has eluded me for so long. Whether I have chased it away or run away from it is incidental to the reality, which is that I have not yet had the pleasure of my father walking me down the aisle. But lest you think me unromantic, I will also admit that I've had my wedding planned since the first time I saw "The Sound of Music" when I was 5. Yes, I know; it's an awfully long time to wait for a husband, let alone a toaster.

So I'm not really against weddings and I don't really prefer funerals. I actually feel pretty confident that someday I will love someone who loves me back and my father will much too gladly hand me over. And when that time comes, my friends had better have their checkbooks ready.

I need a lot of stuff.

—◆—

STANDING IN A LONG LINE at the theater last week, wondering how anyone could have agreed to a date with the idiot in front of me, I started playing a little game to pass the time. I started examining the couples around me to determine if they were married or dating. I've always said wedding rings should be mandatory on both parties, as a courtesy to the rest of us.

Two minutes into the game I was a pro, because the contrasts were less than subtle. Married people, it seemed, wear the married sign around their neck, not around their finger.

And compared with the couples on a date, marriage looked even less appealing than before, which was no easy trick.

Dating people still flirt, and they're still in that "impress me" stage. They make witty conversation and everything is an anecdote. The woman gazes expectantly at her date while he speaks, as if she actually cares what he is saying — which, granted, at that point she still may.

People on a date are also impeccably dressed, even casually — a single person will spend more time trying to look sloppy than some people spend getting ready for the prom. It is important to look just right, and more important to look like you look just right without trying. Unbeknownst to the daters, however, we all know they've been dressing since noon.

Married people, conversely, have That Look, the look of tacit boredom that sets in, presumably, with the realization that there is no longer reason to flirt. I figured this must be what is meant by the "comfortable old shoe" analogy I've feared all these years. The married couples spoke little and touched less. Occasionally their eyes would wander over their surroundings, but for the most part they just waited in line, almost like they were alone.

And I thought, this is why I'm not getting married. These people are so bored they have transcended restlessness. They have nothing to say to each other, no desire to hold hands. They don't flirt and they don't try to impress, and they probably spent 10 minutes getting dressed. How awful for them; how very desolate and bleak. How lucky for me that if I wanted to, I could flirt with and try to impress a different man every night of the week. Assuming, of course, that I ever left my house.

As I stood smugly in that line, however, having won my little game (especially nice since I was playing alone), this eerie feeling started to overtake me — not like being followed down a dark street, but like I'd totally missed a very important point. To an anal retentive such as myself, the latter is far more disconcerting.

So I looked around again. I watched the daters gaze and flirt and carry on, and the marrieds stand side by side in silence, and it came to me. I remember once telling someone something which was very difficult for me to explain and even more difficult for him to understand, but which I had never quite experienced before. I remember telling him that being with him was like being alone.

Bells went off, people cheered, lightning struck. I finally understood. The marrieds weren't bored or unhappy. They had what the daters hadn't yet found — friendship and trust. They were standing around not talking and not touching because they didn't have to talk or touch. They were perfectly satisfied to be silent with each other, to stand side by side looking out, rather than staring at each other and telling stupid stories. They were content just to be together. And I envied them.

For those of us who cherish our alone time and in fact prefer it, to find someone who makes us feel just as comfortable as when we are alone is the ultimate match. I think I'm finally learning that those married people weren't to be pitied. They were the lucky ones.

And they didn't need rings to prove it.

I REMEMBER BEING SICK as a kid. We'd get to lie on the couch all day, watching game shows until the soap operas came on and it was officially nap time. I still can't watch "The Price Is Right" without getting all weepy and nostalgic for the chicken pox. Of course, back then I was sharing the couch with at least three of my brothers, who insisted on getting sick with me so they could snatch the attention from my clutches.

In case you hadn't noticed, sickness in an adult is nothing like sickness in a child. Sniveling, crying and complaining, while somewhat annoying, are at least expected in children.

I think much of the bad behavior in sick grown-ups stems from the realization that we can't just stay home and watch TV. It's way too complicated. Staying home now means screwing up the lives of everyone you work with. Either someone has to do your work while you're out, for which you will pay dearly, or no one will do your work while you're out, for which you will pay dearly — the classic "lose/lose" situation.

And despite my loathing of gender discussions, there are differences between men being sick and women being sick. I'm not even going to try to explain why. I'm just saying it is so.

A guy, for instance, complains of a headache. When it is suggested that he take something, he shakes his head with that "serious integrity decision in progress" look and says, "No. I don't like to take pills." Well, macho man, I know I'm going to love listening to you whine for the next four hours, you bet.

Women take medicine at the first sign of malfunction because we don't have time to waste. We must deal with bosses, husbands and kids, whether we're sick or not, so we might as well be not. We selflessly forgo those philosophical issues with which men stuggle, summing it up in three little words: "Give me drugs."

I went to the doctor for a migraine. I knew what I needed. I arrived on time and sat patiently for an hour. I then went up to the reception desk and vomited. This effectively conveyed to all concerned that I would wait no more. They gave me medicine and sent me home.

My boyfriend, on the other hand, got a cold on Monday. By Wednesday he was worse. On our way home from dinner I suggested he stop at the store to get some cold medicine, and he grimaced. I told him he wouldn't even have to park — he could just slow down, and I would jump out. Still pouting and in his best childspeak, he mumbled, "I could use some soup. Progresso. Chicken. And some Vicks. And maybe some juice." At that point I was looking for a pen. As I finally left the car, he called out, "And I don't have any tissues..."

It's not that men are babies. We all want attention, and we all curl up in the fetal position. The problem is that while we still get as sick as we did as kids, the sympathy isn't as readily available anymore. Being sick now is a whole new ballgame.

So here are the new rules, gentlemen. If you are sick and you won't take medicine, then you can't whine. If you will at least attempt to heal yourselves, then you may whine a little. And if I'm sick, don't follow, "Hi, honey, how are you feeling?" with "What's for dinner?"

When you're sick we will stay up all night with you; conversely, don't assume that when we're sick it's a good time for you to go out with the boys. Oh, and lose the theory that a cold is worse because you have it. It isn't.

Oh — and if we're sick together, home from work and curled up on the couch, don't even think about snatching that remote. I was pretty handy with a Giant Tinkertoy in my day... especially against sick, defenseless boys.

—⁓—

COMMUNICATION BETWEEN THE SEXES is a constant challenge. What we say and what we mean are often two different things, and what is said and what is heard are often two different things, providing about a dozen possible interpretations to any given sentence. Some sentences, like "I love you," often inspire such a quandary that they are often simply omitted from one's vocabulary. I'd assumed it was a dilemma peculiar to humans.

The recent acquisition of Decker, a golden retriever, suggests to me that the problem is not exclusive to us after all. Judging by the manner in which he and I communicate, either the problem transcends species or this puppy is every ex-boyfriend I've ever had, reincarnated into a cute ball of fur with teeth.

I will acknowledge that, yes, Decker is a male. And yes, I probably have some unconscious belief that a male dog will protect me and a female dog will steal my boyfriend. I also believe that having confessed those sins, I should now be forgiven and we should just move along to the issue at hand.

That issue is the very real possibility that dogs and men share a genetic aversion to understanding what they consider unpleasant concepts. And don't get me wrong; I'm not saying men are dogs, "stud" delusions aside, because that could imply that I am a female dog, i.e. bitch, and I would resent that. I wouldn't deny it, but I would resent it.

All I'm saying is we should examine whatever it is that put "puppy" and "love" together in the same song title.

Recent research, in the form of a comprehensive survey of my girlfriends, has shown that what is said is rarely what is heard, or what is meant. "Will you come over tonight?" is cloudy and often misconstrued as "Will you marry me?" when what is meant is "I can't put the storm windows up by myself."

Conversely, the much simpler "Please don't call me any-more because I don't want to see you" is often met with a puzzled, "What do you mean?" What do you mean, what do I mean? WHAT PART DON'T YOU UNDERSTAND?

It's hard to say what you mean and have someone under-stand it as you both said it and meant it. Now try it with a dog. They not only have a similar power of selective interpretation as men; unlike men, they can use that power without punish-ment — because unlike men, there is really nothing you can withhold from a puppy to show him he did something wrong, unless you can hide your house.

Decker has forced me to reassess my whole speaking pat-tern. I have been forced to completely eliminate my favorite expression, because "bite me" has taken on a whole new mean-ing. Also, and this may have nothing to do with the fact that he is a male, and you will recall that you have already forgiven me that bias anyway, but he consistently thinks I mean "yes" when I say "no."

While humans battle with such simple phrases as "trust me," Decker has the darnedest time with "go potty," which he interprets as "run around in psychotic circles and eat moss." Another problem area is "get down!" which in puppyspeak evidently translates to "Jump on my legs and tear my stockings." "Get your bone" sounds just like "chew the comforter," and "go to bed" obviously means "eat my shoe."

We may have stumbled onto a pattern. This dog hears me when I speak because he looks at me and reacts. The fact that he reacts in a totally unrelated manner to what I said may someday be effective in deciphering this whole human-speak situation. It's just a matter of learning the code. I can actually foresee a day when I will say to a man, "I like that tie," and he will wash the dishes.

In the meantime, however, men and women will continue to struggle with "I love you," and Decker and I will continue to struggle with "go potty." And I will remain firm in my blind conviction and stubborn belief that the two phrases are not, in fact, related.

—⚡︎—

Cooties

GUESS WHAT I JUST FOUND OUT? I just found out that men have been afraid of us! Do you believe it? Us! Meek, little ol' us. They've been afraid of women.

There was a recent article by a *Wall Street Journal* reporter addressing these fears, which evidently sprung from the specter of affirmative action and its potential impact on their lives. Fortunately for men, the writer concluded, their fears were unfounded, since the program has not been the obstacle they expected. Golly. I bet you guys are breathing a pre-e-e-t-t-ty big sigh of relief, huh?

This particular article, which was written by a, yep, man, suggested that "just a few years ago, men complained bitterly that competition from women...was imperiling their career climb and job security." It featured the story of a guy who was angry that he might not get his promotion strictly by virtue of his sex — can you imagine? Society discriminating against people because of their sex? Unheard of!

Anyway, he got his promotion, prompting him to conclude that obviously "endeavor, not...gender, is the best road to advancement."

Obviously. Of course. There really could be no other conclusion drawn there, right? There really could be no other explanation for the fact that 95 percent of senior managers in Fortune 1000 companies are men. No other reason. Absolutely none...except for the obscure possibility that maybe, just maybe, THE PROGRAM DIDN'T WORK. Hello, hello, anybody home? Are you people listening to yourselves?

Now, in fairness, I understand that men have ruled the world for more than a few years now. And I even, to a point, understand why. Back in the old days, not like before TV but more like before fire, men did the outside work and women did the inside work. Why? Simple. Men are stronger. It's not a good thing or a bad thing. It's just a thing.

Women were physically incapable of taking out a T Rex, and because we didn't want to sit around and do nothing — besides, of course, propagating the species — we started doing the dishes. And therein we settled into a routine which has continued, lo, these many years. Many were the summer evenings when I stood at the sink, washing dishes for eight people for the third time that day while my four brothers took turns cutting the grass once a week.

The tradition continued when day jobs were invented, because many were again based on physical strength, and because women, as far as men could tell, were pretty content being moms and staying home. And women very well may have been content, since they didn't know the options at that point, which was essentially because there weren't any. I understand all this. I'm not trying to rewrite history.

Today, however, we have lawnmowers that move when you look at them, not to mention women who can benchpress their dates. Technology has finally, generally speaking, leveled the physical playing field in the workplace. That whole strength thing, therefore, just isn't as impressive anymore.

Today women go to college just as men, and we now have day care, freeing us up to work outside of the home. In short, there's nothing men can do that women can't. Except possibly lift a car. But then again, men still can't have babies. And do we even want to go there, really?

This desire to hold onto the power and the money is somewhat understandable, based as it is on a three-billion-year tradition and all. But come on, guys. Let it go. We're here, we're smart, we're talented, we're educated, we're motivated, and we want in. The general affirmative action plan may not have produced the results we wanted this time around, but surely you don't think we're going to stop there, do you?

Because if you do, and if you think you were afraid of us before, then I've just got one thing to say to you.

Boo.

—∞—

I'VE GOT A POP QUIZ for the women in the audience — guys, you can go do whatever it is guys do on Sundays. I'm sure it's pretty important. Hahaha. Kidding.

Anyway, ladies, here we go. You have to listen to the question, analyze the information, and give me the correct answer. Ready? OK — what's wrong with this picture?

"New Hair & Makeup — Fast, Fast, Fast!" — "Waiting a Good Man Out — So He'll Come In from the Cold" — "35 Guaranteed Ways to Get Him to Notice You" — "Does He Keep Putting You Down with His Yammering Criticism?" — "Men Love Mysterious Women — 7 Ways to Become One!"

These are all articles in a national women's magazine. And you know what? They're not about women. They're about men. We're not reading about ways to improve ourselves or educate ourselves or make ourselves better so that we'll be happier, healthier women. We're reading about how to do it so we can get the guy.

And I'll tell you another thing. Search though you may, rarely will you find articles in men's magazines about "How To Please Her In Bed," or "No Butts About It — 10 Ways to Really Turn Her Head," or "Will the Clooney Cut Catch Her Eye? 10 Sexy Coifs for the Average Moe!" And if you do happen to find them, the headlines are sure as hell not screaming from the cover. They're buried in the middle somewhere.

So why don't we see these stories? Because men don't feel the need to change themselves for us. Society taught them they're OK no matter what. We're the ones who've traditionally been assigned the chameleon role because, hey, men want things a certain way. And a woman without a man is like, what? How about a goldfish without a dentist?

And it's not just magazines perpetuating this "men-as-center-of-universe" theme. Many allegedly women-oriented ploys are just covers, deluding us into thinking we count but are really meant for men. Beauty contests spring to mind. Or swimwear. Or Victoria's Secret catalogues — don't even try to tell me you get to it before he does.

Or how about the wedding ritual, which ostensibly spotlights the bride? Women give the bride presents like lingerie and cooking utensils, all of which will surely please the groom. Men give the groom alcohol and another woman, which will presumably not please the bride. And this is fair...how?

Just once I'd like to hear about a mid-afternoon bachelor party at the home of the best man's mother, where the groom gets silk boxers and a nice towel set. Just once.

Men are great, but we should come to them as partners, not Play-Doh. No wonder there are still so many problems related to gender and equality. For all of our efforts to be the best we can be, there remains a shadowy directive that we can do it as long as we remain attractive and desirable to men.

Maybe it's time we looked at men from a new angle. Maybe it's time we start modeling some of their beliefs — like the one that tells them that getting the woman is not one's primary necessity in life. Or the belief that self-improvement is for the benefit of, yes, the self.

Women have traditionally been led to believe that if we could find the right haircut, the right exercise, the right makeup, we would find a guy and be happy. Popular culture still reflects that belief. But you know what? I have scraggly hair, flabby thighs and pretty bad makeup, and I found a guy anyway. And it didn't even matter if I did.

And you know what else? I'm not always happy. All that

stuff — looks, clothes, guys — had nothing to do with anything. We make ourselves happy or we don't. That's what we should be reading about, how to make our lives better. Because from what I can tell, it's not a natural ability for all of us.

OK, ladies — "Learning to Live with His Fetish," "He Might Sit Up and Take Notice If You..." What's wrong with this picture? That's right.

We're not in it.

—✺—

SINCE IT'S APPARENTLY not pathetic enough that people today are afraid to talk to, seduce, or even make eye contact with each other, and that personal ads are mixed in with employment ads, and that dating has become a second job for many of my generation, there are now companies that will, for a price, provide a resume on the next person you ask out to dinner.

They will examine your potential date's criminal record, employment verification, driver's license, civil records, educational documents, and credit history, as if he were interviewing for a position. This from a state that can't even trust itself not to fall into the ocean.

There's probably a very decent premise buried way down deep in there, but frankly there's a part of me that finds the concept somewhat revolting. Do you want to date people as they are, or as they were in a past life that for most of us is just that — past? Today it's our school records; tomorrow it could be former lovers. Yikes.

Sure, it's a handy tool in business. Who wouldn't want to know if someone had a history of theft before hiring him as a bookkeeper? But credit checks on someone with a cute butt? Are you kidding me?

Who among us hasn't bounced a check here or there, or been late on a credit card payment, or defaulted on a student loan back before we knew it mattered for the next 80 years? I mean, that's what I've heard about defaulting on a student loan. People tell me. It's not like I did it myself.

But what if I did? What if I defaulted on my loan, and, say, got arrested at 16 for throwing stones at moving cars to prove I had a better arm than any boy my age, and, for instance, lost a job because my boss was a jerk and in a moment of blind fury I decided he should know?

So what if I did? Those are the kinds of things that make us into the people we are, but they are also the kinds of things that you share with someone one at a time, through the growth of a relationship. That's how trust is built. We do stupid things. We learn from them. We grow up. But those things stay on our records, and apparently those records are never sealed.

Most of us have secrets, things we've done that we're not too proud of, things that are painful to share but need to be shared with people we love because sharing them puts them where they belong — in the past. But those secrets don't define us as we are today and shouldn't be used against us. We are today what we are today, not what we were yesterday.

Bringing my past to the present before dinner is not my way of building trust, but in keeping with the trend, I've worked out the scenario just in case.

"Hi. I'd like to go out with you sometime, and thought

I'd save you some cash. Here's my resume, annotated for the short-attention-span crowd.

Youth: I was an uncoordinated child. Fell down the stairs a lot, broke my glasses. I said my first swear word at age 4, and liked it. I was fishing with my brother one day and accidently pierced his ear with a bad cast. He didn't like it. Middle school — threw a mean softball. Thought I was a boy. High school — discovered real boys. They didn't, however, discover me; spent way too much time listening to Barry Manilow.

College through today: discovered work. Didn't like it; did it anyway. Also discovered alcohol. Didn't like it; did it anyway. Until, at least, I discovered that I preferred having friends. Dated some losers; dated some nice guys. Had many jobs due to low tolerance for idiocy. No major bad debts; many major bad judgment calls. Pretty confident that there's not as many to come since, like most people, I learn from my mistakes."

So what do you think? Did I get the job?

—∞—

CAN YOU BELIEVE EVERYTHING you read?

Think about it. If you can't watch the person saying what he writes, can you be sure it's true? I say, no. People generally need to see body language to fully interpret what's being said, and the written word just doesn't allow for that. At least, most of the time.

Online dialog is an exception, since unlike mere words on a page, it has at least attempted to fuse body language into conversation. When something is humorous, for example, people respond with "LOL" which means "laughing out loud." If their team scores a touchdown, they write "Yea! We scored! (arms waving wildly)." Get it? They translate what their body is doing.

The problem there is honesty. I mean, I guess you could get bored in the middle of an online conversation and write, "Yeah? Really? (yawning, arms folded across chest)." Most people are too nice, however. And of course a serial stalker isn't going to share that little biographical tidbit over the Net: "Hi, I'm Steve, and I like dogs (looking up your profile)." So it has its down side, but the concept is still a valid one, and one I happen to enjoy.

Body language speaks volumes, whether you're witnessing it or describing it, because since we don't always communicate honestly with good ol' English, our bodies compensate by giving away every little lie. It's actually kind of irritating, when you think about it. But it's also enlightening, if you know how to read it.

I've therefore compiled some sample interpretations of body language. I'm obligated to state that they are mine and mine alone, and in fact my boyfriend and I actually disagree on one important point. Can you imagine? My boyfriend and I disagreeing? Already ("looking totally baffled")?

Anyway, he says that only a change in body language means something. If I sat down with a man who was relaxing with his elbows on the table and he then folded them across his chest, symbolically shutting me out, then he probably didn't appreciate my company. Of course, he could have put his elbows on a wet spot, too ("chuckling at the memory").

My view, however, is that if he knew he was meeting with

me and didn't like me, his arms could have been folded when I first sat down and stayed that way except maybe to scratch himself. His position never changed, yet clearly he wasn't happy. Of course this would never happen in real life because everybody likes me ("looking really smug").

But regardless, body language exists, and here's how I read it.

- If you're at a restaurant and your date rests his head in his plate, he's bored.

- If you're talking with someone who continuously rolls his eyes, he thinks you're an idiot. Or he has a really bizarre facial twitch and you really just have to feel sorry for him.

- If a man's at the movies with a woman and she crosses her legs, chances are she's not too interested (either in the date or the movie — I'm not saying it's an exact science, OK?) If she folds her arms and crosses her legs, she probably can't wait until it's over (the date or the movie, all right? I shouldn't have to say this again.)

- If she folds her arms, crosses her legs, and then does that Gumby trick and crosses her ankles, the date's probably over and you should take her home before she gets stuck that way.

See how this works?

Body language is universal, and sadly enough, you just can't get it with the written word. Heck, even I have to explain things I write sometimes, things that wouldn't need explaining if people could see me say them. Or if they were just a little brighter.

Oh, I'm sorry. Now that was unnecessary. It's so unlike me to take potshots at people like that. I'm really quite embarrassed.

I mean that ("head thrown back, laughing hysterically").

—⚏—

"RUBENESQUE" WAS HOW I WAS described back in my teen years, an insult based on an artist whose trademark paintings depicted relatively plump, ivory-skinned women. I was definitely well-rounded, and I wasn't just ivory — I was transparent. The other girls sat next to me in gym class when they wanted to feel thin and tan.

When I grew up, then, I decided to change. I dieted and laid out in the sun, dieted some more and burned some more, and became "Twiggyesque" leaning toward "skin-cancer-esque." And through it all, not much changed. Oh, sure, maybe I wasn't the target of social scorn I once was, but I wasn't any happier. I wanted to be, but I wasn't.

So fast forward to the present. I recently read an article that suggested many women are bypassing the whole panty-hose effort because it's more comfortable to go bare-legged. In that article some hotshot fashion babe said, "Awful, just awful. I don't know what the world is coming to. Not many women have legs perfect enough to go without stockings."

She goes on to recall the good old days when well-dressed women wouldn't be caught dead without stockings because, God forbid, they might show their bruises, varicose veins and cellulite. And what's worse, she complains, without pantyhose, our butts jiggle and underwear lines show.

So what's my point? Here it is: It's absurd, the whole thing.

I finally get it. Nobody should care about this, and I can't quite determine who the problem is. Is it men, for demanding that women hide their imperfections by any means possible so we'll be more attractive to them, or is it women for allowing ourselves to be dictated to? As loathe as I am to admit this, I think it's us. Maybe if we didn't care so much, men wouldn't either.

And the truth is, women are worse than men when it comes to judging women. Take my "maven of misogyny" example — I'd bet a paycheck that she'd beat any guy to the punch when it comes to pointing out another women's varicose veins. I figured this out in high school — "You think you're Casper? Sit next to Maggie!" Women are vicious.

Why is this? Why are we so critical of each other, so intent on looking "perfect"? If we're covering up flaws to get a guy, here's a little news flash — when you get one, he's going to see them. And if we're hiding them from other women, we've got a problem. I mean, if I'm wearing control-top pantyhose under dress slacks in 90-degree heat to win the approval of my own gender, then maybe you'd better just shoot me.

I don't have perfect legs. They are translucent, and I simply won't risk cancer for complete strangers anymore. They're somewhat flabby, and I've got a little cellulite going on the thighs. I've got the occasional varicose vein, and my legs bruise if I even think about walking into the corner of the table. OK? Now that I've admitted this, can I go bare-legged?

If I don't care that my legs aren't perfect, why should anybody else? Why should I be afraid to walk into the grocery store in full flaw gear? Have we nothing better to do than criticize each other? People wonder why our young girls lose their self-esteem; maybe we should be looking at ourselves for that one. Maybe we should stop defining "beauty" in terms of body type. Maybe we should lighten up a bit.

Do you know what beauty really is? I'll tell you — confidence. Being comfortable with and confident in yourself is attractive. Some of the most beautiful women I've ever seen are, at first glance, not "perfect" — but they're happy with themselves. Ruben's women were beautiful because they thought themselves beautiful. It was as simple as that.

"Rubenesque" is no longer an insult. In fact, I'd say it's a goal.

—⁂—

LOOK AROUND AT ALL THE HAPPY couples you know (OK, both of them) and answer this simple question: Do opposites attract? When one person says "Up," does the other say "Down"? Does one say, "I need affection" while the other says "You know, I think touching is highly overrated"?

It's an interesting premise, if it's true. Do we innately search for someone with qualities which, combined with our own, make us whole? Are we fascinated with what is different from us? Or does this attractive guy with a cute butt just coincidentally like to clean?

My own pet theory is that we're all so darn competitive that we find partners who don't pose a threat. For example, if I aspire — or would give my right arm — to be a great writer, I'm not going to seek out men who can write. It's the "Neurotics 'R' Us" theory of attraction. We simply want to be the best at what we are. Whatever that is.

You see examples everywhere you look. Shy folks marry

the gregarious type, which, when you think about it, makes perfect sense. If both were shy, it'd be an awfully quiet 50 or 60 years; if they were both outgoing, nobody would get a word in edgewise.

Similarly, if both people are morning people, there's the risk of never getting invited to parties ("It's only midnight, and the Smiths are sleeping in the corner again!"), and if both are night people there's the danger of beating each other up searching for the snooze button on the alarm clock.

However, if you have one morning and one night person, you'll be on time for work and get home from the party before irreparable social damage is done.

My boyfriend and I have a great system. He's both a morning and a night person, meaning he is perky at 5 a.m. and midnight, and I'm a noon person, meaning I'm usually pretty coherent right around lunch. We've got the bases covered, although he does spend an inordinate amount of time being perky by himself.

Oh — speaking of pet theories, I've noticed similar tendencies between people and their dogs. Isn't it always cute to see a 6'4" bodybuilder walking his little Chihuahua? Not that there's anything wrong with that, but it does look funny. One would expect a huge guy to have a Rottweiler, if not a small bear.

And then there's the man to whom my dog and I have pledged our eternal yet apparently hug-free loyalty. When I feel the urge, I have to physically show Ralph where his arms are supposed to go in order to achieve mutual participation in the hug. He's simply not a hugger, and I can live with that. My dog, however, can't.

Talk about irony! It's not bad enough that poor ol' Iron Man got stuck with a cuddlebunny girlfriend; he also now shares quarters with the world's only moody and downright sensitive dog. I blame myself. I coddled him and cuddled with him and talked to him like the poet I believe him to be. But I've created a monster.

Yep, the boy's gotta have it. He therefore blocks the doorway until he is hugged. That's all. "No shirt, no shoes, no hug, no service." And these aren't quick little pats on the head, either; he burrows into your chest for minutes at a time. The boyfriend actually schedules them into his day.

(Isn't it amazing how this whole "men/dog" thing keeps resurfacing? And I'm not even trying!)

So anyway, those are my theories, but who knows? Do opposites attract? And does it even matter? I guess, based on my experience, that I'd have to say "Yes."

My boyfriend, of course, says "No."

—✕—

THE MUSIC OF SOME OBSCURE-to-anyone-over-20 band pulsated in the background, the sun beat down on my pre-carcinogenic freckles, and I was blissfully napping as young men in shorts and baseball caps sauntered around offering drinks and hors d'oeuvres.

A thirtysomething woman's fantasy? Yeah, maybe in someone else's life. In mine it was just another graduation party, at which I was just another guest. Of the parents.

Observing the gathering, throughout which the young hosts sprinkled some Kiss and Grand Funk Railroad just to be sweet (or snotty, now that I think about it), I couldn't help but study their faces and reminisce about my own such coming of age which, contrary to popular belief, was not all that long ago. Well, OK. Define "long."

Anyway, I also couldn't help but notice that we were looking at each other with a mixture of pity and envy. The graduates pitied us because we're old, and we envied them because they're not. And suddenly I wanted to be 18 again more than I ever wanted anything in my life.

Actually, however, it wasn't so sudden, as I blushingly recall my collection of 1970s discs. Yep, I'm pathetic. When those television commercials want me to pay $29.95 for what in the store would cost 10 bucks, I, weenie-like, call and order it, every single time. They know me by my nickname, for gosh sakes.

My collection generally covers all the bases, though; rock (Blue Oyster Cult is king, although I still don't know what the name means), disco (the Bee Gees were *so intense*!) and the traditional "Music to Cry Your Eyes Out to After a Bad Date," or love songs. Yes, I have them all, from the Bay City Rollers to REO Speedwagon — and I know all the words. "Billy, don't be a hero....." I started humming passionately.

I was rudely awakened from my reverie by a cute young graduate providing a decidedly unappreciated reality check, asking about the whiner blasting from the speaker. In a rare karate flashback, I swept him into a headlock and whispered, "That's Peter Frampton, cupcake. Mr. Frampton to you."

So I'm a tad overzealous. What was it about the 1970s that evokes such an overwhelming feeling of nostalgia every time I hear the music? While I can rewrite history all I want, the truth is it wasn't the best of times for me; I was naive, insecure, too smart, and a fashion nightmare (remember gauze shirts? Still have one.) It meant growing pains, unrequited crushes, and trying to find out who I was, and why. No, it wasn't the best decade of my life.

If only I could go back and do it again, I lamented to an unsuspecting fellow guest, knowing what I know now, things would sure be different. No bad career decisions, no bad boy-friends, no bad diets. I'd do all the right things and make all the right moves with all the right people. And I'd never, ever perm my hair.

But watching these kids, it occurred to me that maybe that's why I loved those days so — because I didn't know everything. Maybe it's the innocence, the naivete that I miss.

I loved the 1970s. It was the last vestige of youth, of no responsibility, of no decisions to make, hearts to break, mort-gages to pay. I'll never forget that era, but as I watch this next generation begin its journey of a lifetime, I thought, go get 'em, tiger. It's your turn. Because the truth is, I just don't want to rock and roll all night and party every day anymore.

It would interfere with my nap.

—✲—

I WAS IN THE CARD STORE RECENTLY making a jackass of myself as I am inclined to do, laughing hysterically at those cards that I wish I could write, when I came across one I hadn't seen before: "If they can put a man on the moon, why not put all of them there?"

When I recovered enough to form a thought, the thought

was indeed unpleasant. Aside from the fact that I would really miss many of them, what would a planet be without men? A planet of women? An involuntary shudder coursed through my body as I admitted what I had only surmised in passing over the years: Women scare me. I probably have one girlfriend for every 10 male friends, and the ratio is decreasing proportionately over time.

Maybe because I have four brothers, or because that cheerleader slammed me into a locker in the ninth grade for what I can only assume was looking at her wrong, but women have always intimidated me in a way that men just never will. As a child, I learned to deal with it as any good victim would; if a girl didn't bother me, I didn't cry. If she did, I did. Not exactly "Beaches," is it?

There are several reasons why befriending women as an adult is so tough. Many are busy with jobs and husbands and/ or kids and don't have time for new relationships. Or they're involved with someone and don't have time for old friends, let alone new ones. If they're not involved, they probably want to be friends but are really busy and are not inclined to make time for new relationships that don't involve, for lack of a better word, sex. We get close to other women at work but when the job ends, usually the friendships do, too.

It is also no doubt due in part to childhood, when the virulent seeds of jealousy and insecurity are planted in little girls which ultimately convince us that other little girls are put on this earth solely to steal our boyfriends. My immature response would have been, lady, I don't even know why YOU want your boyfriend. But I'm growing up now. Maybe it's time for a truce.

There is simply no reason for us to not have girlfriends. The old school days are over, and having the same last initial is thankfully no longer the only basis for association. In fact, chances are good that you're not going to have very much in common with the friends you make as an adult, and chances are better that it's not going to matter.

I met my best friend at karate class a few years ago, and I remember thinking, oh great. She's bigger than me and she likes to fight. This should be a treat. I thought she was mean, and she thought I was flighty. But while both were pretty accurate assessments, I found that after several months I could finally talk to her without breaking out in a cold sweat, and she could respond without rolling her eyes and walking away. We've been friends ever since, though no one quite knows why.

She makes brownies from scratch, and I make student loan payments. She decorates her house for Halloween, and I hide my car and pretend I'm not home. She cleans her kitchen every day and I, um, don't. She gets a cart in the grocery store, and the pizza people know my voice on the phone. She's raised a beautiful daughter by herself for a decade and a half, and I had to return a kitten after two days because it just wanted too much from me.

In short, she shows me how to be a grown-up, and I remind her how to be a kid. And we both adore those stupid greeting cards. So while I may not particularly want to be alone on the planet with them, I am learning, finally, that women are not to be feared.

Even if they can beat you up.

ALL'S FAIR IN LOVE. ANYTHING GOES. Take your best shot. At least, that's what I always believed. No one had to tell me how to play the game.

Apparently, however, therein lies the root of perpetual unhappiness: We simply weren't playing right. This discovered, two women determined all the things we must do to catch a guy and live happily ever after. "The Rules" tell us exactly how we must behave to make a man marry us.

It's a sort of "Men Are from Mars, Women Are from Stepford" philosophy, directed at women whose reason for living is to get married. As for the rest of us, the ones who actually have a life, the premise of the rules merits some thought. I won't cover all of the rules for lack of time; I only plan on being here another 60 years or so. But we'll hit the highlights.

The stated purpose of the rules is "to make Mr. Right obsessed with having you as his by making yourself seem unattainable." Putting aside the stalking issue here, we're told to play hard-to-get because biologically the man is the aggressor, and we must let him take charge. Evidently it's our only chance.

Women therefore must make a few minor changes. For instance, and I quote, "Don't act like a man. Be feminine. Don't tell sarcastic jokes. Don't be a loud, hysterically funny girl. Be quiet and mysterious, act ladylike, cross your legs and smile. Don't talk so much. Wear black sheer pantyhose and hike up your skirt to entice the opposite sex!"

It's easy. Just watch what I do, and do the exact opposite.

But wait, there's more. The book suggests that because our primary life purpose is attracting men, we should always wear sexy clothing that hides our hips, surgically correct physical flaws, and never, ever leave the house without makeup, even to go jogging.

I personally can't count the men who've stopped me while running to ask me out. Well, hold on...with all that sweat and makeup running down my face, maybe they were saying "help" me out. Who knows? Anyway, you just can't tell where you'll meet Mr. Right, and you should always be prepared.

Be prepared, also, for the inevitability of him waking up before you've had a chance to metamorphose one morning and saying, "Hi. Have we met?"

And this one really hurt: "Men prefer long hair, something to play with and caress." (Guys? Care to jump in here? Can you say "Halle Berry"?) Apparently it doesn't matter that short hair is easier to wash and dry or that my hair is very fine. We're girls! We don't want to look like boys! Yeah, they're right. It's the hair. It's not like the breasts give it away.

Following the instructions on how to get him is, naturally, advice on how to keep him, which requires a few more minor personality revisions. We must overlook his faults, build up his ego, tell him how good he looks and see things his way. Parenthetically, most guys I know would be happy with this for about 45 seconds, and that's being generous to accommodate some of the slower ones.

It's at least acknowledged that "it takes a lot more work to be a rules wife than an ordinary one." And although they might have to try "seeing a therapist or joining a support group" to handle the stress, they say it's worth it in the end — "the end" being, presumably, when your head explodes.

Maybe I'm just not getting it. All I know is I've pretty much always been happy, with or without a guy, because I like myself and I can be myself. I don't need a score pad to keep track of the lies. I play this game the old-fashioned way.

And the rules are, there are no rules.

—⁓—

"DOGS ARE PACK ANIMALS," the trainer patiently explained as I imagined motorcycles revving in the background. "Pack animals know their position at a very young age. The problem here is that Decker believes he is the alpha dog. He believes he is in charge of you. You, in effect, have not earned his respect."

Well, thank you very much, Mr. Show-Him-Who's-Boss. Are we talking about my dog or my boyfriends? Red-faced and humiliated, I nevertheless maintained my calm, cool façade.

"I give him treats," I cried. "I am the treatmaster! How could he not respect me?"

"He doesn't respect you because you treat him like the superior. You let him lead you — or, from what I've seen today, drag you — down the street. You pet him, groom him, feed him and love him without making him work. You give and give without asking anything in return."

Well, duh, I thought. I'm a woman. What's your point?

But I remained polite, as I was taught to do. "What can I do, Your Trainerness? How can this problem be fixed? How can I make my dog stop acting like a man?"

Oops; it slipped out. I couldn't stop it. It just popped out of my mouth like a piece of steak after the Heimlich maneuver. And I couldn't take it back, because from the sudden ice in his eyes, I knew he'd heard it.

"The fact that Decker is a male has nothing to do with the fact that he believes he is superior," he not-so-patiently explained. "The fact that you spoil him rotten has everything to do with it. Correct me if I'm wrong here, but your boyfriends have the same problem with the dog, and your boyfriends — again, correct me if I'm wrong — are male. Leader and subordinate roles are not gender-based. You, yourself, are behaving like a dog. Just a very submissive one."

Or, shut up before you say something else equally stupid.

"What must happen here," he continued after making sure my lips weren't moving, "is a role reversal. You must become the Alpha dog. You must make him work for everything. If you want to pet him, make him sit. If you want to feed him, make him sit. You want to play cards with him, you make him sit. You have to learn to demand something from him every time he gets something from you."

In other words, I have to stop being the way I've been since birth. This, fortunately, was not said out loud. I'm nothing if not a good student.

Now, we've all heard the "men are dogs" jokes; heck, I've even written some. But this new theory has opened my eyes a bit. Maybe we're all where we're at because of training — by whomever — and not because of gender. Maybe it can, after all, be changed.

I'll admit it's not easy for me to ask something in return for giving. I learned from the generations before me, whose women gave without receiving and whose men took without giving. It wasn't a good thing or a bad thing, really; it was just a thing. It was just how it was done. But now it has to be undone.

My paradigm, therefore, has shifted. If someone continually gives without asking anything in return, the recipient of those gifts is going to start feeling a little powerful. And those of us who've traditionally embraced that dynamic can either master some new modes of thought, or accept it and be dragged down the street. Either way, it's time to accept responsibility for our own training.

So I'm in obedience school with my dog. I'm learning to assert myself and to ask for something in return for my love and affection. I'm learning to be, if not superior, at least equal for the first time in my life, which is a pretty darn good feeling.

And that's why they call me the leader of the pack. Vroom, vroom.

—∞—

Tick, Tock

VERY FEW THINGS FRIGHTEN ME. Spiders larger than the average tomato; people with guns and no visible respect for life; the words "We need to talk" coming from someone I love. External things, things outside of me. But the inside of me is pretty safe, so not much scares me.

Well, there's one more thing. Kids. Kids scare me to death.

I recently had one of the more self-examination-inducing experiences of my adult life, spending a weekend with three adorable, intelligent children. For those without kids, I'll try to relate the experience in words and images us childless folk understand; for you parents out there, all I can say is, wow. Way to go. I'm a little speechless here. I mean, wow.

The first thing that struck me about kids was the completely unadulterated honesty with which they approach life. It's not that I'm such a big liar, necessarily, but I'm just not used to being with people who are absolutely unafraid to say what's on their minds.

For instance, the child on my lap was examining my face, and pointing to the pimple I spent 20 minutes covering up, she asked, "What's that, Miss Maggie?" Once I got over the humiliation of being busted by a 3-year-old, I still had to answer.

"Well, sweetie, that's a little blemish," I mumbled.

"But it's not very little, is it!" she giggled in delight.

"No, dear, it sure isn't. Go find Mommy now."

I didn't feel quite so bad upon overhearing her brother's chat with their uncle.

"What's on your face, Uncle Ralph?"

"That's a beard, honey."

"What's a beard, Uncle Ralph?"

"Well, it's hair that grows on my face."

"Why is it there?"

"Because I like it."

"Why do you like it?"

"Because it looks good."

"Can I have one?"

"No, you're too young."

"Why am I too young?"

"Go find Mommy now."

Oh, the questions! There's nothing like a conversation with a toddler to confirm why you'll never be on "Jeopardy"— "Why do birds fly?" "How does the oven work?" "Why don't you have a baby?" "How long is five minutes?"

And while kids aren't afraid to admit they don't know everything, I've spent the better part of 15 years covering up that very fact. So instead of answering "I don't know" to one of their more difficult queries, I offered a ridiculous explanation in vocabulary most adults wouldn't understand in the blind hope they wouldn't discover I was a fraud.

Gone was any semblance of dignity and respect. I looked down at their sweet young faces after some such soliloquy and saw a look which I'm quite sure translated to, "What a bozo! Let's go play."

Kids are very literal, too; I'll have to revamp my entire vocabulary if I ever become a mom. I once made the mistake of telling them I couldn't play because I was pooped, and you can just imagine the turn that conversation took.

And speaking of imagination — I'll have to take a class. My sister-in-law told the kids a story, making it up as she went, and I was as mesmerized as they were. She knows all the songs, too. The only one I remember is "Itsy Bitsy Spider," and that's only because it traumatized me for life. I still believe it was the basis for a "Twilight Zone" episode.

It's so very frightening. These little people completely entrust us with their lives, and I'm afraid I'm unworthy of that trust. I'm afraid of my own inadequacy, of being wrong, of making a mistake. I'm afraid I'll let them down and not be able to protect them from hurt. I'm afraid of not being a good mom. So despite my theory on fear, I guess it's not the kids I'm afraid of, after all.

I guess, after all, that it's me.

—⚏—

"HE'S BEEN UP ALL NIGHT!" I whined to my mother. "As soon as I fall asleep he's crying to go out again! I know he doesn't feel good, but darn it, every time he has to go, I have to get dressed and go out in the cold. You can't tell me that having a baby is harder than having a dog."

"Well, honey," my mom replied, irritatingly mom-like, "I believe I can. For starters, you don't actually 'have' a dog."

Thus continued the Great Debate over children and dogs. It's not that my mother doesn't love my dog, because she does. Well, she says she does. Anyway, we tend to get into it when she gets wistful for real grandchildren, and I tend to make excuses because I'm terrified.

"You know, raising a dog is no picnic," I shot back. "He's a big responsibility. Heck, when he was a puppy I had to watch him 24 hours a day — do you think it was easy?"

"No, dear, of course not. I can't imagine," she said. What she didn't say, but really wanted to, was, "I only had six kids, you moron." Encouraged by her concession, however, I forged on. "How hard can babies be? They wear diapers. They wake up and you go four feet and change them. You don't even need slippers, for Pete's sake."

"I know dogs aren't easy." she replied, patiently. "It's just that dogs and babies are different." What she didn't say here, but again really wanted to, was, "And if I have to tell you that, then maybe you'd better not reproduce anyway."

Well, duh. I know they're different, but there are some similarities, too. People even talk to them the same. They see a cute little baby and murmur, "Hello, you sweet thing! Coochie-coochie cooooo!!!" — and then they say the exact same thing to the next puppy they see! Tell me it doesn't happen.

What's worse, while holding a friend's baby recently, I unconsciously started scratching his head. This set off warning buzzers from every direction, I don't mind telling you. I was more than a little embarrassed when his mom came back to find me petting her child.

So what else? Babies and dogs both cuddle. Of course, when you're done cuddling with a baby you're not pulling hairs out of your mouth. And they both love you unconditionally, at least until they can feed themselves. Which means that all dogs and most boys will love you unconditionally. Hahaha. Kidding. I have four brothers.

Anyway, each also has advantages. Dogs don't cry, for example. Of course, children don't bark. Well, one of my brothers did, but I think it was just a phase. And dogs don't need diapers. Of course, children will someday use a toilet. Well, one of my brothers...wait. Never mind.

Let's see. Dogs don't have homework to remind you how little you know. But kids don't look at your shoe as a potential meal. Dogs don't put you through the agony of teen-age dating and the know-it-all attitude that makes me want to put adolescents on an island until they're adults. But children don't look at your leg as a potential date.

So maybe there's no debate to be had. If I can love a dog this much, maybe I shouldn't be so afraid of having kids. Maybe next time, instead of the gentle click-click-click of the dog circling the bed, I'll awaken to the sound of my mother's grandchild mewing in the darkness — the relentless crying of a hungry baby with a wet diaper — the deafening, thunderous wail of an infant with lungs the size of Idaho...(sigh.)

Maybe I'm rushing things. I mean, it's not like my mom doesn't have five other kids, for crying out loud. And heck, it's almost spring; it's not even that cold out anymore. And the dog's beginning to feel better anyway. And...

—⁓—

A RECENT STUDY IN NORWAY suggests that unhappy people do better work than cheerful ones, who overestimated their own ability, underestimated the complexity of problems and opted for the easy way out. Sad people, on the other hand, were less confident, and so they looked deeper and found more creative solutions.

The researchers cited the example that Einstein was depressed when he came up with the theory of relativity. Parenthetically, I can't help but wonder what was going on in the life — and the head — of whoever invented calculus. I do know I'd like to throw him a Zoloft.

Anyway, I have a new respect for some of my past employers. I now know they weren't really the jerks they pretended to be but only attempting to make me do better work. You sly devils, you. Who would've thought you actually had my best interests in mind the whole time you were making my hair fall out?

Along those lines, I also have a new theory about women in the workplace, and it is this: People will soon be treating us just a little bit better, and wanting us just a little bit more. Why? Because this study suggests, in a nutshell, that PMS makes us better employees.

However, because said condition lasts in most cases two weeks per month, here's a little reminder to hang at our desks for the other half of our adult lives when good moods threaten. Although based merely on personal observation, I hope it will offer the occasional reality check for those rare moments when we are lulled into believing society might actually be coming around.

- 95 percent of management of Fortune 1000 companies are male.

- Women don't earn as much money as men doing the same jobs, if they are able to obtain those same jobs.

- Women remain the primary caretakers of children and home despite equal time with men in the workplace.

- Women are worshipped for their ability to gain 60 pounds over a nine-month span and then scorned when they don't lose it in month 10.

- Menstrual cramps are not universally accepted as a valid complaint, but jock itch is.

- Parents are now in some places punished for their children's crimes. Most children who commit crimes come from one-parent homes. Most one-parent homes are headed by a mother who must work to feed her children, leaving them unsupervised — which can now land her in jail.

- Most intelligent, witty, attractive and financially secure men are married.

- As for the rest, single men are still socially more accepted than single women, and...

- ...single dads are sexier than single moms.

- Men hanging out in a bar look like they're bonding. Women hanging out in a bar look like they're hunting.

- "Men Are From Mars" spent a gazillion weeks on the best-sellers' list, confirming that men have always and will always behave badly and there's nothing women can do except learn to live with it.

- The president of the United States was sued for sexual harassment...

- ...and then re-elected.

That should to it. This should quell any urges we might have to break out in song at the office. And while men continue to control the business environment, I don't mind telling you how proud I am to be able to make the workplace more productive and successful. Nor do I mind the fact that this affliction, for which men have historically committed us to mental institutions or dismissed altogether, can finally be used to benefit them.

Now go on out there, ladies, and knock 'em dead.

———

WHEN I WAS YOUNGER, a priest told me a sin was only a sin if you knew it was wrong and did it anyway. It was a kid's way of knowing what was right. My powers of rationalization being what they were, I'm pretty sure I was perfect back then. How could I not be? It was easy.

Lately, however, it seems the right thing is getting a little more difficult to identify — let alone do. Reason No. 87 why I don't care for this whole adult thing.

On a recent flight, the attendant offered me a soda, and before I could snatch it out of her hand because my ears were popping so badly I thought my head would explode, I hesitated.

I thought, hmmmm. I'm in an airplane, so the bathroom is the size of a shoebox. I'm in the front, so I must wade through 600 people to get there. And the person sitting next to me weighs 300 pounds, so a carbonated burp will ruffle his nose hair. The ear-popping problem no longer seemed so bad. Therefore, I decided to graciously decline the soda. I really said that, too; "I'll graciously decline the soda." What a grown-up thing to do. Good for me.

As adults, we tend to do the right thing despite the degree of personal pain or sacrifice it will cause us. This is inversely proportional to how we behaved as kids. Back then, the degree of pain was way more important than the degree of right. If we happened to do the right thing, it was because it was coincidentally less painful than the wrong thing.

My parents recently sold the family home. It was a tough choice, but one that had to be made. They shouldn't have to take care of a big old house, and whoever was supposed to circulate the schedule for us kids to come home and help out apparently nodded off. So they got a smaller place. And we're all a little sad about it.

We whine and complain that we no longer have a home, despite the fact that we've all lived elsewhere for 15 years. We wonder where we'll sleep when we all come home to visit, when in reality the last time we were all in the same house at the same time, one of us was still in grammar school. It was a tough choice, but they did the right thing.

And what of our generation? Do we make the right decisions at the expense of personal desires? Hell, yeah. You can't tell me that anyone without kids has a minivan. Or that people who don't have a family history of heart disease give up salt. Or that just once, you wouldn't rather say, "You'd like me to do...*what?*" instead of, "Sure thing, boss."

But don't confuse the right thing with the safe thing. That's another difference between then and now. Back then, the right thing was the one that would work. It's not that easy anymore. Committing to a relationship doesn't guarantee you won't get hurt. Selling your home doesn't necessarily mean you'll be better off. Biting your tongue at work doesn't mean you won't get canned someday anyway. Not that this has happened to me, necessarily.

I used to believe in the safe thing. I took the easy way out — staying single because it's too hard to combine lives, renting instead of owning because it's too much hassle to buy, staying at jobs I didn't like because, hey, I'm going to die someday anyway. But I'm beginning to realize that life is a little more than biding time until death.

There's a limited amount of time here to be happy and, in pursuit of that goal, there's going to be some pain. It doesn't mean we did the wrong thing; it means the right thing, as far as we can tell, is worth some trouble. Being grown up means knowing how difficult the right thing is and, despite the rationalization, doing it anyway.

Anything less, really, would be a sin.

—⁓—

WHY DO WE ALWAYS WANT what we can't have?

Despite the zillion books that probably address this very subject, I sit on my couch for countless hours pondering this and other age-old questions, like what is my purpose in life, who is going to feed me tonight, and why oh why do we insist on being attracted to people who are not interested in us while the people who are interested in us are viewed as the emotional equivalent of toe jam?

Given the choice between Lassie and Mr. Spock, we unerringly choose Mr. Spock with the blind hope that someday, with enough love and devotion and total abdication of any feminist thought we might ever have had, he may show an emotion.

We've all gone out with people who dote on us, treat us like royalty, hug us without being asked, and ultimately we would prefer that they return to their home planet. After three dates Gentleman A wants to marry me, while Gentleman B wakes up with the "And you are...?" look after six months of living together. And Gentleman B is the one I want.

Why do we do this? Why do we devote ourselves to the pursuit of the unattainable, to the exclusion of the attainable? It's as if we look for situations that will enable us to question our self-worth. Maybe if we could target some of the reasons we do what we do, we could begin to stop doing it. And I think we should be looking way back.

I'm not blaming society, necessarily, and I am certainly not blaming my parents; they obviously didn't know then what we know now. For instance, how could they have foreseen that the rosy, sunburned cheeks on their red-haired daughter would someday metastasize? And while they blanched somewhat at the dermatology bill I sent them, they know I don't blame them.

More to the point, I believe that nursery rhymes may have

had more than a passing effect on my sanity, and that they should at least be examined, if not regulated.

Remember "Itsy Bitsy Spider"? It's the spider from "The Twilight Zone." It won't die. "It's Raining, It's Pouring" is the endearing tale of a man who knocks himself out cold in a storm "and didn't get up in the morning," meaning that, unlike the spider, he did die. (Mom now tells me it's "didn't get up *til* the morning," which would have been good to know about 30 years ago. Can't unring that bell, Mom. You'll be getting your facts straight before you'll be baby-sitting any future grandchildren.) And then there's Mr. Athlete Jack, who takes a header down a hill, cracks his skull open, and waits while Ms. Girlfriend Jill dutifully follows.

This explains, in order, my fear of spiders, thunderstorms and commitment.

"The Ugly Duckling," however, is the king. This poor thing starts off pathetically homely, and inside of four minutes is transformed into a beautiful swan. I, however, had to listen to that song until I was coherent enough to ask my mother what exactly her point was, because what I was getting was, "I know you're not the prettiest thing, honey, but someday, after years of insults and way too much time alone wondering if a butter knife can draw blood, you could be a late bloomer and worthy of living! Won't that be great?!"

Maybe that's why we go after people we can't have. Maybe it's like the old saying, "I wouldn't go to a party that would have me as a guest." We think the people who adore us must somehow be flawed, so instead we seek validation and love from people who won't give it to us, thereby confirming our self-image and allowing us to go about our business with a sense of, well, we tried. See what happens?

It's like the dog chasing the bus. Catching it could really hurt.

I think we have to learn that just because people love us and treat us right doesn't inherently mean they are stupid. And that people who say they don't want a commitment usually don't. And that, bottom line, we don't really always need someone anyway.

Yikes. If they thought the dermatologist was expensive, wait until my parents get the therapy bill.

—⁓—

SOME CO-WORKERS AND I RECENTLY had a lovely lunch throughout which we debated the pros and cons of marriage. The guys discussed the pros, because they're happily married. My girlfriend and I discussed the cons, because we're not. Married, that is. Well, we're not cons, either, unless there's something she's not telling me.

But as the boys so delicately put it, we single women sure are guilty of something. "Husband-hunting," I think they called it, in that totally enlightened guy way. And they made it sound like a crime. So we did what any good feminists would do — argued until we were blue in the face about how men have no concept about what women are about and therefore we'll never get married. (Translation: "This is a stupid game and I don't want to play anymore.")

We tried in vain to explain that some women just don't need marriage, and it's actually pretty ironic that heterosexual marriages are the norm when men and women are so obviously different. But they couldn't seem to grasp the concept of marriage as an option, taking the stance that women date for one reason, and one reason alone. Women, apparently, are all DWI — Dating With Intent.

And if we're not husband-hunting, we're male-bashers, because everyone knows there's no such thing as a single woman just hanging out living her life. I mean, if we're not out there in active pursuit of Mr. Wonderful, we might as well just kill ourselves, right? No wonder men run from us, if that's what they think. I'd run, too.

But maybe that's the problem. Maybe they don't know what we want, or maybe we don't tell them because maybe we're ashamed of ourselves for wanting it. After all, if we've waited this long to get married, why bother? And besides, it's so un-'90s to want a commitment. It's so *needy*.

But after lunch, when Gloria Steinem left my body and joined my girlfriend in search of someone with a few more guts, I wondered why I took such offense to their assertion. And I came to the undeniable conclusion that it was because I want to get married. There, I said it. I want to meet a guy someday and fall in love. I want to be a wife. I want to have kids, and I want them to have the best possible home, and I know myself — and my shortcomings — well enough to know that the best possible home will involve someone besides just me.

Why are we so afraid to admit to this? Because we can't win, that's why. If we're this old and still single, we're slammed for being too picky, and in the next breath we're slammed for being desperate. Does that strike anyone as even remotely paradoxical? How can I be picky *and* desperate, for Pete's sake?

I may want a husband, but make no mistake about it — I could've had one. I could've had five, for that matter. But if it's not right I'd rather be alone. And when it is right, I want marriage. Case closed.

It can be tough, admittedly, weeding people out of the ol' marriage pool. I always feel mildly awkward asking someone on the second or third date if he ever wants to get married. It requires a certain delicacy, a certain panache.

"No, you arrogant prick. I'm not saying I want to marry you. I don't even know if I like you. What I'm saying is, I do want to get married someday. So if you know that you don't, tell me now before I decide I do like you, because frankly I no longer have the time or the energy for sport dating. Now, how about that dinner, big guy?"

So I confess — I'm guilty of DWI. I guess someday, some poor sap is going to have to put that rope around my finger, tie the knot, and sentence me to life.

—⁂—

I'VE FINALLY DISCOVERED what separates us from other life forms, and it's not, as I previously claimed, our opposable thumb which allows us to hold a pen. Rather, it is our incredible gift of imagination and the way we use it to rewrite history.

And I'm not talking about hopelessly demented bozos who've convinced themselves that they really were quite attractive in their younger days. I'm talking about generally sane and rational individuals who've somehow come to believe that the most traumatic events in their lives weren't so awful after all.

Who among us, for example, hasn't looked back on a

relationship and managed to turn the reasons we left into the reasons we want to return? "Oh, sure, I know he was moody and slovenly and kind of stupid, but it was so charming!" So you get back together and after a few weeks you realize those qualities were not, in fact, charming at all.

Why do we do it? Why do we need to glorify the past? It made us what we are today, so why can't we just accept it as it was and move on? Are we that ashamed of it? Does remembering the bad times remind us that we're not perfect? Or do we just have way too much time on our hands?

A song recently came on the radio that I hadn't heard in years. I said, "Oh, honey, listen! I haven't heard this song in years!" I then got all misty and nostalgic for the good old days, until my boyfriend, Mr. Sensitive, said, "Um, sweetheart, wasn't that song popular right about the time you quit drinking and couldn't leave your couch for six months except to go to the bathroom?"

"Well, yeah," I replied, somewhat testily, I think. "What's your point?"

His point, which was well taken about three weeks later, was that we can't deny our histories. Doing so is an insult to ourselves and everyone who played a part in them. I see that now; the struggles we go through play a major role in shaping the people we become, and to try, for whatever reason, to soften them — or erase them — is an injustice. To deny the bad times is to deny the good.

So no more, gosh darn it! It's time to stand up and say, hey, that period of my life really stunk! I've done some really stupid things! Yeah, that's it! This guy treated me really badly! I'm sure not proud of my behavior at that party! Boy, I was a real jerk back then, huh?!

See? This is almost fun, in a disturbed kind of way.

Now, don't get me wrong. I'm not saying dwell on this stuff, because that in itself is a real social turnoff. But if we forget how much some things hurt, or how hard they were, we run the risk of making the same mistakes. And at this stage of the game, it might not be only our lives we will affect.

The good news is, despite the past we may be stuck with, the future is still ours to script. That ability actually makes the past useful, because we can only make a better future if we have a basis for comparison. We certainly can't make things good if we don't or won't remember how they were bad.

Boy, it's hard, though. It's so much easier to pretend things were better than they were, to use our wonderful imaginations to protect ourselves from pain. But I know that if I want a better future, I have to resist the urge to rewrite my past to make it more acceptable. I have to resist the words that, especially as a writer, are so darn easy to say.

"Pen, please."

—⁘—

I AM, AT HEART, AN APARTMENT DWELLER. A tenant, if you will. Have been all of my life. I never had the sense of responsibility to be in charge myself, and so I lived by other peoples' rules. And they were always the same, from when I was a kid to, um, last year, actually: "No loud music. No parties. No swinging from the light fixtures. And absolutely no waterbeds."

In that spirit of tenancy, therefore, I willingly shared my

last flat with a little mouse that lived in my piano. OK, maybe "willing" is a tad generous, but when I managed to pull myself off the ceiling after his first public appearance, I agreed he could stay. Heck, he was just another transient like myself. And besides, he made the most amusing little screech every time I hit the G sharp.

This is what people who shun responsibility do. They share their lack of responsibility with others. It's like a little support group, helping us through the occasional pangs of guilt associated with never having to fix a broken appliance.

So you can imagine my surprise when I woke up one day to discover myself a homeowner. And after all these years, it's still sinking in that no one is telling me what I can and can't do. Oh, sure, my boyfriend might weakly claim the house belongs to both of us, but come on, honey. You could hit our plumber with your car and not recognize him. I, conversely, have him on speed dial.

I reflected on all of this the other day when I went down to the basement and found another mouse. I couldn't believe it. Is it something about my housekeeping? (Could that possibly be?) When I pulled myself off the ceiling, however, I couldn't help but notice that this one was dead.

Feeling a little safer (although a little sad, as well, at the passing of a member of God's great kingdom), I ran upstairs to find a cat. (No use in two members of the great kingdom having a bad day, I always say.) There was not one in sight, however, probably not inconsistent with my stance on cat lovers. This is presumably what is meant by "payback."

I knew then that I had to go back down there and take

care of this myself. My boyfriend works during the day, so it's my job to keep the house free of animals and other non-rent-paying creatures. Except for the dog, of course. Oh, for Pete's sake, there're a few spiders, too, OK? Happy now?

At any rate, I donned the triple-thick neon-yellow gloves you're supposed to wear when cleaning the bathtub (of course, I just read that on the box, after cleaning for six years with my bare hands. No wonder I have no fingerprints left.) I then grabbed the garden shovel and an entire box of trash bags, and down I went.

There I was, feeling every bit like Linda Hamilton in Terminator 2 (but not looking like her, as if that needed clarification), and darn if the thing wasn't gone. Poof. Disappeared. He wasn't dead when I found him. He was sleeping. I found the one rodent in the history of the world who naps like I do — anytime, anywhere, for any reason.

Now that ticked me off a bit. Sure I felt bad when I thought he was a goner, but my house will not be used as a hotel. First he makes himself a nice little nest in the corner, next thing you know he wants cable. Well, it's not gonna happen, not on my watch. This house has rules.

So I hunted the little critter down, cornered him, and without even flinching, I did what I had to do. "Listen up, buddy. There will be no loud music. No parties. No swinging from the light fixtures. And absolutely, positively, no waterbeds!"

—◊—

"HAPPY BIRTHDAY TO ME, happy birthday to me, happy birthday, dear Maggie, happy birthday to me!"

Yep, it's my birthday (if my singing didn't give that away) and I'm now officially on the downswing to the big 4-0. I was just sitting here drinking my coffee and waiting for the hysteria to kick in, and guess what? It didn't! I didn't fall apart, I didn't get crazy. Nothing. It was just another morning.

It was almost anticlimactic, I don't mind telling you.

It's as though, dare I say it, age doesn't matter anymore. Or maybe it's just getting harder to measure. In the past, when I'd read something in the paper about somebody and it said, "So-and-so, 35, ..." I'd think, wow, that person is way older than me, as if seeing the age in print somehow made it a reality that didn't belong to me. The age in the paper was always older than the age I was at. Even if they were the same.

Maybe it's a holdover from childhood, when those ages in the paper really were older than me. Rarely did you see a story about "Tommy Brown, 6, ..." It just didn't happen. We don't do that much newsworthy stuff when we're kids. So all those years reading ages just confirmed that everyone was older than us.

That image lasted well into my 20s. Even people younger than me seemed older than me. Maybe it was the criteria I used for judging maturity, which included a) height, b) marital status and c) income. If people were taller than me, married, and/or made more money, they were older.

Now, though, when I see "Jane Smith, 35, ..." I think, hmmm. My age. Wonder if I know her. (Sigh.) You know you're old when, huh?

But I'm not old, gosh darn it. The ability to face reality doesn't mean I don't like to play Candyland. I'm the age I'm at, that's all. One day I was 5, another day I'll be 60 (I hope). Time marches on, but that doesn't necessarily mean I'm getting trampled.

It does mean, however, that I've temporarily shelved my dream of a sports car because a child seat wouldn't fit in the back.

And that I'm buying groceries for more than the next 12 hours — and using a cart.

And that I gripe sometimes because really, does anyone ever have enough baking supplies?

It means that I'm now the one asking, "What the heck is that, anyway? Music? And do they have to play it so darn loud?"

And that napping is now a luxury instead of a daily necessity.

And that somehow, the needs of the people I love have taken priority over my own — despite the battle I'm reasonably sure I put up for many, many years.

It means I'm a little more aware of how lucky I've been, and a little less bitter about things that didn't go right; a little more conscious of how other people feel and a little less inclined to hurt them just because I can. I'm a little closer to understanding how really quite nice it is to be around.

And through it all, the true spirit of "birthday" transcends any ridiculous fear about getting old. It was the day my mother gave birth to her first daughter and made sure right off the bat that I didn't have my brothers' big ears. It was the day I came screaming and whining into this world with nary a clue that I would never stop. It's the anniversary of the day I was born.

And everyone knows what that means, so come on, people, sing along with me.

"I ge-et pres-ents, nyah nyah-nyah nyah nyah!"

—⚭—

IT SEEMS LIKE EVERYONE has a hobby. Some people collect stamps, some do needlework. I never really had one, though, except for maybe my dog. Now, however, as demonstrated by my shopping-bag full of them, I collect pictures. It's as though I just discovered the technology. Of course, I just recently discovered umbrellas, too; I've never been what you'd call "cutting edge."

But that's why this picture thing is so much fun — that, and our new "flagship" camera (read: it looks really cool and cost a lot and can do a ton of stuff except you need an engineering degree to know how) which we've been using to the point of abuse. I mean, heck — a pastime is one thing, but Decker, the poor dog, has actually learned to vogue.

We didn't have a lot of pictures when we were growing up; maybe that's why they're so important now. And we never had a photo album, which might explain the shopping bag. There was the Bible, with our various locks of hair and report cards and baby pictures from the hospital which made us look like we had fins, and there was The Drawer.

The Drawer was my mom's little shrine. It held pictures of my grandparents and my parents' grandparents, pictures of my parents when they were kids, and pictures of us kids as we grew up. Oddly, though, there was only a few of each, except for my oldest brother, the boy wonder.

They must have mistaken him for some famous child model

or something, because there are pictures of him doing everything from sleeping to barfing. The kid was a trained seal. Then of course my next brother came along, at which point my parents must have started getting bored because there are only about six pictures of him. By my arrival they had apparently lost interest altogether, because there's only two of me.

Faced with the accusation, my mom merely remarked, "I'm sorry, honey. But look at your poor sister — after five other kids, it's a wonder her birth was documented at all."

"Well, that's comforting, Mom," I replied. "I feel much better. Wait — I have a sister?"

Anyway, over the years The Drawer became full and our collection was moved quite unceremoniously to a box, which had the added benefit of four sides to gather around as opposed to The Drawer's paltry little front. Kneeling at it one at a time looked somewhat like paying respects at a casket and was about as much fun. I mean, how much pleasure is there in mocking someone's picture if they can't hear it?

Be that as it may, I'm now getting a little nervous about where we're going to put our own little collection. Even if we only take a roll of film per month (and that's being way conservative, I might add), we're looking at tens of thousands of pictures over the next decade or so. Where do they go?

My boyfriend naturally has the logical solution; sort them by the date that is conveniently (and somewhat intrusively, if you ask me) located at the bottom of each picture and catalog them by month and year. So what if most albums hold 200 photos and we've got 8000 of just our dog. None of this box and drawer stuff for my guy, huh, babe? You ol' sentimentalist, you.

But that's OK. We can have albums. It doesn't mean I can't keep some of the special ones in with my socks if I really wanted to, for old times' sake. It just means I've finally found a hobby, I'm finally approaching that cutting edge. And I'm getting pretty darn good at, I don't mind telling you, although it helps to have a willing model.

Come on, Deck…that's a good boy…say "cheese"!

—✎—

I Do. No, I Don't. OK, I Do.

REMEMBER NERDS? They wore pocket protectors and glasses and had bad haircuts and weren't quite physically developed enough for anything more strenuous than studying. We mocked their short-sleeved button-down shirts, stuck "kick me" signs on their backs, and generally made their lives miserable. They were the antithesis of the yuppie image.

Now, however, we're marrying them, and not because we're desperate, either. We're actually choosing them. And the reason is this: guppies. "Geeky, upwardly-mobile professionals."

Really, I made that up. I actually speak here of the fish. Apparently scientists were struck by their remarkable similarities to humans, so they studied their mating habits in an effort to help explain the process of evolution. What they discovered is almost humbling in its simplicity.

It seems that, absent any behavioral information about their, er, dates, female guppies chose flashy, attractive males. In a situation involving danger or fear, however, they went for bravery over beauty. Better to end up on the arm of a less-than-natty dresser than on a plate with a side of chips, I always say.

Anyway, make that small leap into the human arena, and it makes perfect sense. Cute boys are fun to play with and all, but over the long haul, we want more.

What was that? (Sigh.) Oh, all right. I, Maggie Lamond, do hereby make the following disclaimer of my own free will:

"This column is based in theory only. It in no way describes my fiance, who is more handsome than John F. Kennedy Jr., and who is not now, nor was he ever, a geek in any sense of the word, except where said word is construed as a good thing." That about cover it, babe? Great.

If I may continue, I was suggesting that guys who were geeks in high school are ending up with the great women, and I think the reason has to do with maturity. Good-looking guys never grow up. And when women grow up and start wanting adult relationships, we're going to seek out someone for whom "Hello" is not a preamble to "What's in it for me?"

It's not really the cute guys' fault. Popularity is important to kids, and it's usually tied to looks. Good-looking boys get used to being the center of attention. The less stylish group — the nerds — don't need to be the center of attention, as is evidenced by their complete disregard for what's hot and what's not. They're comfortable with who they are.

As young girls, we're attracted to good-looking boys because we're looking for self-esteem and acceptance. As we mature, however, and find those qualities where we should have looked in the first place, i.e. ourselves, our perception of what is attractive matures with us. We no longer want a man who can boost our ego, but one who can control his own. We wake up one day and think, "Gosh, those glasses are really quite sexy." Or, "Look at those floods — that confidence makes my knees weak!" You just want to hug these guys, don'tcha?

Boys with the "kick me" signs learned way back what was important: sensitivity, inner strength, compassion. What made them outcasts back then is precisely what makes them so desirable now. When we're puking from morning sickness or working late at the office, their initial reaction is, "How can I help?" not "Will you be able to cook?"

I'd like to offer an apology to all of the boys from high school whom I wouldn't date because they just weren't cool enough. And on behalf of all the women who've ended up with a pocket-protector guy, thanks for forgiving us and waiting for us to catch up with your maturity. You're so special, I think they even wrote a song for you.

And they called it guppy love.

—m—

"YOU DON'T HAVE TO GO HOME, but you can't stay here."

That was my favorite expression back in my bartending days when I wanted patrons to leave. It defined my control over my space, which was a little area behind three feet of wood that no one else could touch. When everyone left, I could clean and organize and make it just the way I thought it should be.

That sense of power was something I was never afraid to use; my drink-mixing abilities at the time definitely overshadowed my people skills. And while those days are long gone (shhh — if you listen closely, you can hear the collective sigh of relief from the local drinking community), the attitude remains. We've all got a certain space that we stubbornly defend, a place that is ours and ours alone.

Maybe it's a room in your home that's off-limits to everyone else. Maybe it's your car, which almost defiantly reflects your true personality if not your true cleaning habits. Maybe, if you're a dog, it's the spot at the end of the couch where people better not sit if they know what's good for them, or, actually, if they don't want a buttful of hair.

Or maybe, as in the case of someone very close to me who wishes to remain anonymous because he disagrees with me, it's the desk in the kitchen.

It's a simple desk, really; a little one-drawered number attached to the end of the counter that holds miscellaneous stuff like bills and stamps and take-out menus. But this simple little desk clued me in to a great insight of life — a person's space is his space. It's one of the weirdest things I've ever seen.

For instance, to clean off his desk, this anonymous person will take everything that doesn't belong there (according to him) and put it on the counter next to the desk. That's all. Bye-bye. Dog brushes and battery chargers and screwdrivers mix willy-nilly with coffee cups and spoons, while the desk is perfectly clear. I can almost hear him mumbling, "You don't have to go home...." It's really almost frightening.

But that's how people are. They don't care where the stuff that's invading their space goes, as long as it goes. When someone is talking to me with his nose 3 inches from mine, I really don't care if he falls off a cliff as long as he takes a few steps back.

So I guess I understand, and I'm learning to work around it. This "someone" was going through his watch collection drawer the other day and pulled out a book that some bozo (oops!) had erroneously tossed in there. "This doesn't belong in there," he said, and laid the book on top of the dresser. And walked away.

"Well, it doesn't belong there either!" I was about to shout after him, until I realized the futility of it all. It's not about where things go; it's about where they don't go. It's about retaining some degree of control over one's special places, and that's really not a lot to ask.

As family dynamics change, you have to learn to share and give up and give in because that's how relationships work. Your space, then, becomes both a reminder of how far you've come as well as your last vestige of autonomy. It is the place that is — still — yours and yours alone.

Yep, that's what it's about, I think to myself, glaring at the disks and computer cords and Post-Its that have become annoying patrons of my comfortably nostalgic space, that little spot behind three feet of wood. And as I begin the overwhelming chore of cleaning off and organizing my desk, I still have the same old thought.

"All right, time to go. You don't have to go home, but you can't stay here."

—⁊⁊⁊—

MY DANCE PARTNER AND I were practicing our newly acquired dance steps recently, because we are, in fact, the queerest premarital couple in the history of the world, and we were listening to the oldies station because the stuff we learned doesn't go with anything else, when a song came on that stopped Ralph "Fred Astaire" dead in his foxtrottin' tracks.

"Hey!" he exclaimed. "That song doesn't belong here!" He was really miffed. They may as well have announced, "Yes, big guy, this song is for you, and you know why? Because you're old!" He was beside himself. Good girl that I am, I took it upon myself to comfort him.

"There, there, now," I said, soothingly. "This song obviously means a lot to you. Tell me all about it...since I wasn't actually born yet."

He looked at me with this rather pitiful expression, a mixture, I think, of longing for the old days, of stark acceptance of the fact that his songs are on the oldies channel, and of the dawning realization that somewhere in there I managed to insult him. When I was pretty confident that he'd picked up on that last point, I continued.

"Of course it belongs there," I said. "It was popular 25 years ago. The fact that you still remember it is a testament to your keen memory, not your youth. It also means, I believe, that you hit puberty way before I did."

And so ended our dancing. Maybe I should have been more sensitive, I don't know. Maybe it's not easy for some people to accept the inevitability of aging. I don't mind it myself because, confidentially, being a juvenile all these years has been just a tad tiring. So maybe I can help ease the transition with some warning signs which may indicate you're being tapped off the dance floor of youth.

You know you're getting old when...

∞ You're the one glaring at the people speeding down your residential street, instead of the one being glared at.

∞ You no longer yearn for the days when you were 10 pounds thinner — you yearn for the days when it mattered.

∞ Your seasonally trendy clothes have been steadily replaced by timeless classics because, darn, that mall is so crowded anymore!

∞ You say things like, "Early to bed, early to rise..." and "Honey, could you please turn that music down?" without batting an eye.

∞ The bare spots on your lawn bug you almost as much as the ones on your head.

∞ You hold a wet cloth and glass of water while someone you love is throwing up, instead of running away to be sick yourself.

∞ The *Sports Illustrated* swimsuit edition no longer makes you jealous. It makes you laugh.

∞ The carload of precocious teen-age boys behind you inspires a sense of disapproval rather than a quick makeup job in the rearview mirror.

∞ You catch yourself doing something your parents did and breathe a sentimental sigh, instead of screaming "AAAAAHHHHHHH" like you would have a few years ago.

∞ You nostalgically inhale the wonderful scents drifting from Victoria's Secret on your way to the cotton undies section of the nearest department store.

Aging isn't so bad, really. I think it's the perception we

used to have of older people that bothers us. They didn't understand, remember? And they just weren't cool, or so we thought. Little did we know that from here on in we've got it made — the power to make choices and the knowledge to use it wisely. What more could we want?

And that's just what I told Fred as I helped him again to his feet. Where we are is where it's at — whether we're rockin' around the clock, shaking a booty...

...or rockin' on the porch, knitting one.

—⚎—

I'M SHOPPING WITH MY GIRLFRIENDS and trying on clothes, and we start talking about guys and stuff, and so I ask the saleswoman, "Are you married?"

"Married!" she practically spits. "Are you crazy?" She nearly chokes.

Although I normally commend such spirit, this was not quite the attitude I expected this time. I was trying on wedding dresses.

Yep, we're finally doing it, taking the plunge, tying the knot, gettin' hitched, biting the bullet for the big M, which in my life has always meant "meatloaf" and inspired about as much enthusiasm. And it's a little different now for both of us. "Terrifying" is actually the word that springs to mind. But we're ready.

How do we know we're ready? It's simple, really, once you get past that whole love thing (which, incidentally, was not simple, really). We've reached the point at which there are no more emotional traumas, no more baggage, no more ghosts. We know each other completely and like each other anyway.

But it's more than that. The question I ask when he goes out of town is no longer, "Will you remember me?" but "Did you pack your handkerchiefs?"

At night I take makeup off instead of putting it on. Slipping into something more comfortable, more often than not, involves sweats. And that's all OK.

Our irritating little habits have gone from annoying to Major Issues back to merely annoying again. I eat the frosting off the cake; he dries each piece of clothing separately. I round my checkbook to the nearest zero; he fits five entries on one line. And that's OK, too.

We can chat through dinner or say nothing at all. We watch each other's shows with only minimal sarcasm. And when we argue, we no longer wonder who can run away faster but whether he might just be wrong. (Did I say "he"? I meant "we." Really.) But it's even more than that.

Our house is now a home. The dog hair on the carpet, which once inspired a certain degree of coziness if not out-and-out warmth, now inspires me to whip out the ol' hand-vac twice a day. The refrigerator is no longer merely a storage spot for film, or the kitchen table a resting place for bills. Who would've thought?

And I'd be lying if I said I wasn't enjoying the whole process. I'm now daddy's little girl again instead of "the one in Syracuse." I seem to possess a certain legitimacy, a maturity, that was lacking in my single days. And — get this — I get to just pick out things for people to buy me! Finally!

Oh, sure, I miss things about being single: the freedom to lie around all weekend (which I still do, but with a certain amount of remorse); coming and going without regard for someone else's needs or schedule (which he still does, but again, with remorse); cleaning the kitchen once a year whether it needs or not.

Yes, that lifestyle will be sorely missed, particularly by the pizza delivery people whose bills I paid.

And it's been rough on him, too. We were driving recently and I said something about kids, something subtle like, "When are we having them?" He slowed down and turned to whisper those three little words ("Get out now"), when a flash of the diamond on my finger reminded him that I'm now permitted to bring this up.

So it's a little scary. It's a big commitment, one which I used to hold in generally the same regard as the woman at the bridal store. But do I think it's the right decision? Do I think we're ready for such a commitment? And do I think it will give me that much more to write about? Well, what else can I say?

I do.

DID YOU EVER NOTICE how you never have enough bath towels? They just don't seem like the kind of thing you buy for yourself. We're down to three, but we're trying to hold out for a little while longer because of, well, you know. The wedding. Or, more specifically, the shower. You see, towels are on our list.

I know, I know. Registering for wedding gifts is like the antidote to surprise. You can't very well exclaim, "Oh, I love it!" when everyone knows you not only picked it out but specified size, color and quantity while you were at it. It was not without a little shame, then, that we took the inevitable stroll down appliance lane with our recording gun and made our list.

This list then goes into a computer to be pulled up by people who love you and want to buy you things. There's even a space for you to leave a message for family and friends — "Thank you for your generosity," "See you at the wedding," "It's my turn." People pull your little list, read your little message and, if they aren't too offended, buy you the stuff you asked for. I kind of like it.

There was a time, though, when I didn't. That time was the first 34 years of my life, when I was buying gifts for everybody else and complaining that I never got any just because I happened at the time to prefer my own company. I vowed never to get sucked into that vicious shower game because it was unfair and downright irritating.

Evidently I've now broken that vow in a very big way, and I'm somewhat embarrassed. This, then, is my apology for everyone who rallied behind me in the old days — I didn't abandon you, guys. I've just been busy. But our idea could still work.

Our idea is based on the premise that many life-changing events occur every day that don't involve marriage or children but are just as worthy of gifts. I know many single, childless people who could use a blender, and so we've gotten together to define what we consider to be valid yet highly underrated shower occasions.

The "S/He Dumped the Loser" Shower: This is an all-too-common scenario for which we should be ashamed of ourselves.

We unfailingly offer our unsolicited opinion about how we disapprove of a friend's current, um, "living situation," until he (or she) finally follows our advice and moves out.

He then finds himself in a completely unfurnished apartment with nothing. I believe our usual response is something like, "Good move! You'll be happy you did it! OK, gotta go!" We have to stop that. He did the right thing by moving out; now let's do the right thing and buy him some cups.

Then there's the "Honey These Things Are 30 Years Old" Shower, which should occur periodically to replenish the stuff you got for your wedding. I realize they could also be called "Anniversary Parties," but you're missing my point here. People need new house stuff after all those years. They don't need new crystal.

And of course there's the "Single And Looking but Need Stuff in the Meantime" Shower, the "Wish I Were Single (and Therefore May Be Single Soon)" Shower, and the "Single and Proud Of It" Shower, all of which I think accurately describe why someone may be in need of household appliances.

We all need things at some point in our lives that we simply can't or don't get for ourselves. Marriage and babies shouldn't be the only occasions we get them — not that getting them at those times isn't a complete hoot because, believe me, it is. I've gotten things I didn't even know existed (mainly kitchen items, oddly enough). But other people need these things, too.

So go ahead, shower the people. Because, really, everyone needs towels.

—✶—

"ONLY TWO MORE WEEKS!" everyone is so keen on pointing out. "Are you getting nervous?"

Ignoring their not incredibly subtle attempt to make me crazy, I calmly reply, "Why, no — I'm not nervous at all! See, when I'm nervous, certain clues unfailingly give it away. I forget things and stutter and sweat profusely which, as you can all plainly observe, is not happening!"

And why should I be nervous, anyway? We're saying vows before family and friends that we've said a thousand times in private. How hard can it be? Besides, we've got all the bases covered. Everything's under control. Heck, I have the caterer on speed-dial. I'm the organization queen.

(Uh-oh; when was that last fitting supposed to be? What if I lose weight or — yikes — gain some? Does the seamstress press it, or do I send it somewhere? And how exactly am I supposed to go to the bathroom? And the veil — am I supposed to hang it in the shower or something to de-wrinkle it? Why didn't anyone tell me not to leave it in the bag for eight months?!)

Yep, we've stayed pretty much on top of things. There's no reason not to, really. If you stay organized, you can avoid the last-minute hassles that happen at other peoples' weddings. We've all heard the stories — groom not showing up, gown being torched in a warehouse fire, best man forgetting the wedding rings. That stuff won't happen to me, no siree Bob.

(Hmmm...Bob ... Bob ... oh yes — the photographer! Did I confirm him? Did I even hire him? What about video — did we decide on that? Are we doing pictures while we get ready, and do I really want anyone to see me then? What about pictures at the church? Outside somewhere? What if it rains? Is there a rain date?)

Nope, that stuff won't happen, because this wedding is planned with a capital "P." We know who's coming, the lay-out of the reception, the rehearsal dinner details (although I don't think I've shared that information with anyone else — I should get on that). And I'm working on directions since half of the guests are driving in from out of town. I just hope I can master that whole east/west problem I have.

(And speaking of driving, what about this limo thing? Do my attendants ride with me to the church? Do my parents? What about his parents? Shouldn't they be included if my parents are included? And if the attendants and our parents ride with me, what about the flower girls and ring bearer? And they'd probably want their parents with them...just how tacky is a bus?)

But aside from that, I should be all set. Well, we still have to get a marriage license. And a kennel for the dog while we're on our honeymoon — shoot! Did I confirm the honeymoon plans? No. OK, I have to do that yet. And I'll have to get my nails done, of course. And my hair. And pick up the wedding rings and attendants' gifts. And we have to find a place to stay on our wedding night because I inadvertently loaned our house to my family.

And we still have to hook up with the priest and organist to decide on ceremony details and find out how the florist can decorate the church and darn it, didn't she want to look at the reception hall again? How could I forget that? And did I remember to tell the band that playing "Old Time Rock and

Roll" is grounds for assault? Did I remember to tell them the date? Who is my band, anyway?

So, um, yeah — what was the question? Am I nervous? No. I'm d-d-definitely not n-n-nervous. Hey — anybody g-g-got a t-t-towel? I'm d-d-dripping over here.

—⁂—

TODAY HE IS MY HUSBAND.

The words sound somehow odd coming from me, as if they don't quite belong in combination together. Like "Hand me the piano." But they're only words, after all; simple semantics. Everything else seems the same. Maybe the only real difference between yesterday and today is the new ring on my finger.

What else, really, could have changed?

I'm still the same happy-go-lucky girl who eats the frosting off cake, the wild-and-crazy babe who panics if she's not on the couch watching television by 9 p.m. I still laugh at my own jokes and make fun of stupid people. I mean, I got married. I didn't have a lobotomy.

But, still, I do feel a change as we brunch this morning with family and friends. I feel as though I'm treated a little differently. I'm no longer sitting at the kids' table, if you know what I mean.

Maybe that's it. Maybe I've finally released my stranglehold on adolescence. There's a certain maturity endemic to marriage which was either buried in denial or absent altogether while I wallowed in what proved to be a marathon single life — a maturity based on commitment which allows me to understand, in retrospect, the difference between playing house and being home.

But it's even more. I feel grounded. Not like for being bad but like when you can't get hit by lightning. It's this safe, confident, responsible feeling, the belief that somebody's on my side, that I'll never again suffer or celebrate alone. The feeling that I finally, finally belong.

Somewhere along the line, "What about me?" became "What about us?" Somewhere through the ups and downs, I realized I'm not happier with just my dog and that marriage is not necessarily the social equivalent of prison — despite any similarity in food. (Sigh.) One thing at a time here, people.

Anyway, I now also understand what I've always sensed but could never quite appreciate. Married people have a wisdom, a bond which, despite my proclamations to the contrary, I envied; a "you and me against the world" kind of unspoken conviction shared by two people committed for life. I envied that trust, so vital and yet so elusive.

It's a tricky thing, trust. All the love in the world won't make you happy if you don't have it. And it's not something you either have or you don't. You have to want it and work at it and earn it and build it. And sometimes it's just easier to be alone than to chance getting hurt, again.

It's like that exercise when you fall backward into another's waiting arms. After you land on your butt a few times, you start looking around to see where he's at, or if he's there at all. Trust is gone, replaced by an overwhelming need for self-protection. And when you've spent so many years building up walls, brick by brick, hurt by hurt, to let them crumble is to go out in a blizzard without a coat.

But then one day you meet someone with the most incredible blue eyes you've ever seen, and you gradually realize that in 50 years you could still talk to him over breakfast, and you take the chance. You find that extraordinary someone who convinces you that life is not always a storm.

And as we begin this tremendous journey, I've never felt at once so afraid, yet so sure. I'm afraid of letting down, and of being let down; of taking for granted, and being taken for granted; of being a mom, and of not being a mom; of losing myself, and of finding myself. I'm afraid of living this dream I've found, and of losing it.

But I'm sure, finally, that it's a journey I want to make, and I'm sure I want to make it with him. Because today, everything is different.

Today I am his wife.

—⁓—

"THE PARTY'S OVER, throw in the towel, the fat lady's singing," my friend told me the other day, suggesting that because I'm married now, there's probably no more "angst" in my life and therefore I might as well kill myself, or at least give up writing. My friend, obviously, is single.

It's not that marriage isn't wonderful, because it is. But we didn't move to Stepford, last I checked; we're still the same very different people we were. Being married just gives us much more time to spot the differences. And I'll admit there was a time when I thought, like my friend, that once you fell in love and got married, everything would be great. No problems. Happily ever after. "I Got You, Babe."

All right, that's enough. If you married people out there will stop laughing and pull yourselves together, I'll get on with it, OK? I used the past tense, didn't I? That's my whole point, already.

For example, it's pretty hard to have someone else around giving input into your life. When you've been doing something a certain way for a zillion years, you can't help but assume the other person's wrong. It's even harder when both people are completely bullheaded...I would imagine.

Each person has cleaning styles and laundry preferences and record-keeping systems and loyalties to grocery stores, and you simply cannot have two completely independent sets of styles and preferences and systems and loyalties and still expect to function as a unit. You have to learn, eventually, to concede some of the control. (Right, honey?)

And then there's the "housewife" issue, which must've been easier 50 years ago simply because women didn't have a choice. Well, I'm lucky enough to have a choice, and what do I get? Conflict. I'm at war with myself, and I'll tell you why.

I was brought up by my parents to go to college and be independent and make a better life for myself than they had. I was brought up by society to believe that being a homemaker was somehow demeaning. So I went to school and had a career and supported myself all of this time.

Now I have the option to stay home, and guess what? I want to. I like working at home. And I take care of the house as payment for that privilege. It's my part. But when the weekend comes around, it's still my part, and I don't want it to be. I want it to be a job like my husband's, with a paycheck and weekends off. I've chosen to stay home, and then resent my husband for it.

I feel guilty for having the choice, ashamed that my choice seems inconsistent with my upbringing, and angry that I feel like I have to defend myself. I can't shake the old mindset, and can't help feeling I'm setting the women's movement back, yet know in my heart I'm doing what I want to do. I mean, wasn't it all about choice in the first place?

And talk about conflict — I belong to a recipe club, for Pete's sake. What do you think that does for my image?

I'm not looking for sympathy, because I'll figure it all out eventually. I'm looking for my friend to understand that marriage can be a wonderful part of the life process, but life issues aren't mollified by that piece of paper. If people don't want to hear about them, that's one thing. But to deny they exist would be a disservice to married people — heck, all people — everywhere. Not to mention it would really torque me off.

So I told her I have my own favorite expression, one that has helped me keep a perspective through the entire process, and it goes a little something like this: "Walk a mile in my shoes."

Angst it the truth.

—∞—

I RECENTLY READ AN ARTICLE about an English tradition in which a couple is rewarded with a side of bacon for not fighting for a year and a day. I couldn't believe my eyes.

I threw it in front of my husband and cried, "Hey! Look at

this! We should do it! We should enter the contest! I mean, who couldn't use a side of bacon, right? How hard could it be?"

And I honestly believed it. How difficult could it be to not fight with your spouse? If you loved someone enough to get married, then what could you possibly fight about? Doesn't being married mean that you're always happy? Of course it does. My husband most certainly is.

So we set up the interview. We were very excited. The contest was ours. It wasn't even fair, really. It was like playing the lottery when you already know the numbers. We sat down with the interviewer, giddy with anticipation.

"Sign us up!" we said. "We want to win a side of bacon! We haven't fought in a year and a day, and we never regret being married! We're the perfect couple! We're always happy, we don't annoy each other, and neither of us has any irritating habits!"

"Well, wait a second..." my husband said slowly, turning to me. "I wouldn't go quite that far. I mean, you know how you never finish a glass of anything? That's kind of irritating."

"Yeah, I guess it is," I replied. "And sometimes, when the bathroom tissue roll is almost empty and I get out a new one and put it on the back of the toilet and you use that instead of using up the old one, I get a little annoyed."

"I know, I know," he chuckled. "And how about your concept of punctuality? People may think something's wrong if I'm not five minutes early, but they think the same thing if you're not a half hour late!"

"Isn't that hysterical?" I said, laughing. "But you know what's really funny? The way you keep stuffing things into the kitchen garbage as if the bag is going to magically get bigger as time goes on! That cracks me up!"

"No! Stop! You're killing me!" he cried, tears rolling down his cheeks. "And here's what else does — the way you order way more than you can eat when we go to a restaurant! It's like you think you're never going to eat again! That gets me every time!"

OK, I thought. It's starting to get a little personal here.

"Oh yeah?" I said, a little hurt. "How do you explain the fact that every time I'm on the telephone, you view it as a prime opportunity to converse with me? Or your almost inconceivable desire to clean the house before the housekeeper comes?"

"I would say that those are nothing compared to your inexplicable belief that the dishwasher somehow empties itself," he snapped. "And then there's your charming inability to distinguish left from right when giving directions."

"A habit which is matched in irritability," I shot back, "only by your lack of desire to watch the road."

"I'll tell you what," he replied. "I'll start watching the road more if you'll stop grocery shopping without a list. The ol' 'Well, we need everything' excuse REALLY bothers me."

It was getting ugly. My husband and I looked at each other, and finally shrugged. None of it mattered, we knew. That's not what marriage is about. What matters is that we love each other and try to be decent people. If we have the occasional argument, it doesn't mean we're not a good couple. It means we're human.

"You know what?" he said, putting his arm around me, "Let's get outta here. We don't even like bacon."

—⚬—

I WAS GOING THROUGH THE BOX the other day, the one that's moved with me since college containing all of my important stuff, and I found some old letters and cards from relationships gone by. As I read them I got all misty and nostalgic, and suddenly I realized something for the first time in the month I've been married.

I can no longer date.

I shared this revelation with my husband, asking, "Did you know this? That you can't date anyone else? Ever? For the rest of your life?" He laughed and replied, "Well, yes, I did." He paused. "You didn't?"

"Of course I did...theoretically," I said, "but I guess the reality didn't hit me until now. I mean, our vows didn't specifically say 'No More Dating Other People.'"

He kind of glared at me this time. "It's implied."

OK, fine. I don't want to date anyone else anyway. It's just hard sometimes to let go of the past, and the older I get, the more past I have to let go of. But since I've always found it helpful to bare my soul to complete strangers, I will take this opportunity to give my deceased dating life a decent burial.

I will share, finally, some of the more profound tips I've accumulated over the years, since it looks like I won't be needing them anymore. I will pass the baton and give freedom to my little black book of experience. I will teach those who are doggie-paddling through the dating pool of life to dive in without getting hurt. As often.

∞ First and foremost, be honest. If, for instance, you want kids someday, you have a right to ask for your date's thoughts on the subject without being arrested for DWI (dating with intent). Your time is precious, and you shouldn't waste it on someone whose life goals aren't even remotely similar to your own. You're not asking for a commitment; you're asking if, somewhere down the road, in the far distant future, the two of you end up together, your partner would share your feelings. If your date gets all nervous and jerky, I've got three little words that usually do the trick: "Get over yourself."

∞ Don't spend your first date with someone slamming your former dates. It's a dead giveaway of how you're going to behave — i.e. badly — when your current becomes an ex.

∞ Women, don't parade around in a guy's shirts and boxers unless you've been together for about 80 years. You may think it's romantic but, generally speaking, he doesn't. A person's stuff is his stuff. And men, leaving dirty clothes around a woman's apartment is not construed as some obscure sign of commitment. It's construed as a sign that you're a slob.

∞ Don't be afraid to say no. If someone asks you out and you're not interested, just say it. "Thank you, but I'm not interested." Practice saying it out loud. "You seem very nice, but I'm not interested." Say it again. "I appreciate the fact that you haven't had a date in nine years, but I'm not interested."

∞ Don't call a former love every three months because you're lonely and miss the good old days. You'll just realize all over again why it didn't work and hurt the other person in the process. If you need an ego recharge, get a dog.

The biggest thing I learned from dating, lo, those many years is that most of us have way too much baggage. We fold up the past like a security blanket and put it away for safekeeping, and that's OK for awhile. But not forever. At some point you have to bring it out in plain view, look at it, and let it go.

And though it's tough, it can be done. My box is now empty.

—∞—

Nine Months, 65 Pounds

"THERE SHE WAS JUST A-WADDLIN' down the street, singing doo wah diddy diddy dum diddy doo, belly so big she could barely see her feet, singing doo wah diddy diddy dum diddy doo…"

Yep, we're soon going to enter the somewhat terrifying realm of parenthood, as demonstrated by my changing body (amusingly reminiscent of Jabba the Hut) and my emotional state (not-so-amusingly reminiscent of "The Exorcist.") It finally happened. Not that I was under any pressure or anything.

There'd been some concern, of course. My sister-in-law approached the baby race as an actual competition (and you can bet that may be a little more than I needed to know about my brother), while my mother developed a charming habit of looking at her watch every time I came home. As if anything's going to happen when I'm visiting my mother.

My mother-in-law handled the whole situation very well, with only a very few impeccably placed sighs here and there, while my dear husband spent more than his fair share of time pondering the possible tax effects of children heading to college as Social Security kicks in.

But everyone can now relax, except, of course, me. I can't relax because a) I really, really liked being a size 3, and b) at the end of all this, an 8-pound person is somehow going to leave me through an exit the size of an olive pit. I've therefore assembled some suggestions and observations for people who are not currently pregnant, to help ease the way for those of us who are.

- Lose the dismissive, "Get over yourself, women give birth every day" attitude. People die every day, too. They still need support. It's not like we're asking for special treatment or anything...wait a minute. Yes, we are. We're growing babies here.

- Fathers, imagine having the flu for three straight months and still having to work, cook, clean, and take care of the kids and dog. Help out. At least *try* to look busy.

- Reading books doesn't cause the symptoms we experience. If that were the case, we'd all have gone through "sympathy pregnancies" in sixth grade health class. The symptoms are real, so don't try to convince yourself — or us — that we've imagined them. Trust me. That head-spinning routine is not a pretty sight.

- Don't blanche at the clothes we have to buy. This isn't a day job that allows us to go back to our regular wardrobe nights and weekends.

- Society likes thin people. Many of us have spent the majority of our lives trying to get or stay that way, so gaining weight — even for this — can be difficult. If you're going to say, "You don't even look pregnant," you may as well add, "It just looks like you've gained 30 pounds." Be tactful. Lie if you have to. Tell us we look great.

∞ Resist the urge to snicker when we're stuck on our backs in the bathtub like turtles. Remember that while the gravity problem that prevents us from performing certain basic maneuvers will soon fade, our memories will not.

Now, don't get me wrong. My husband and I have spent many evenings of late discussing the end of life as we know it, and we've concluded it'll be the best thing that ever happened to us. But I'm definitely not handling the journey very gracefully, because beautiful though it is, graceful it is not. And if it's going to come out kicking and screaming anyway, then darn it, this baby's going to learn from a pro.

"Now I'm so nauseous nearly every single day, singin' doo wah diddy diddy dum diddy doo, so just give me my crackers and get out of my way...singin' doo wah diddy diddy dum diddy doo...

———

"I HOPE YOU DON'T TAKE THIS PERSONALLY, honey," I said to my husband, "but sometimes I just want to run away. It seems that the more pregnant I get, the more I miss being single, and living alone, and not having to take care of anyone but myself, and being able to do whatever I want, whenever I want, with whomever I want."

He looked vaguely hurt for a second and replied, "Why

would I take that personally?" He then shook his head and walked away in his now-signature state of disbelief.

"Wait!" I called after him, "that's not what I meant!" But it was too late. He was gone, presumably in search of that section of the pregnancy handbook that tells fathers-to-be to essentially ignore all the stupid things their wives say during this nine-month period. I'm pretty sure he's made copies and hidden them throughout the house so there's always one close by.

Yep, this thing sure is wreaking havoc on pretty much every aspect of life. I don't know why, exactly, although I blame it on the hormones and that seems to work. It just seems to bring out every element of fear, insecurity, selfishness and immaturity that ever existed. He's working on it, though — hahaha! Kidding. I was actually talking about me.

And just to set the record straight, let's clear up a few scattered areas of apparent concern. No, it's not twins. And I know — now — that when they say it's OK to gain 35 pounds, they don't mean in the first six months. And I also know, intellectually, that this child is not deliberately mistaking my bladder for a park bench.

I also know that I'm really happy to be pregnant. It's just that everyone always talks about how beautiful the process is (and it is, in a theoretical, textbook kind of way), how sexy a pregnant woman can be (which she can, if she's Elle McPherson), and how joyful these nine months are (and they are, particularly if you consider planning any given outing around proximity of toilets to be a joyful experience).

No one talks about the other stuff, the realities and fears that first-time moms can experience. For instance, sometimes pregnant women can't exercise like they used to. I can no longer run or take karate. All I can do is walk, which was always enjoyable with my dog but which now seems painfully like a day job. I walk my dog his two miles, and I walk me my two miles, and I look like the neighborhood moron going up and down the street all day long.

And the closer I get, the more I realize I don't know any of the songs kids like, or the games they're supposed to play, or the shows they're supposed to watch, or the books they're supposed to read. Heck, I have a hard time remembering high school. I mean, sure, I watch Nickelodeon, but it's for "Mary Tyler Moore" and "Bob Newhart." Oh, all right. Sometimes I watch "The Brady Bunch," too, OK? Jeez. Tough crowd.

Oh, yeah, and what is this Barney phenomenon all about, and how come every time I see him, I think fondly of football season and what it must feel like to punt him across the yard? I'd better have some input in that area, that's all I can say.

See what I mean? There's a lot more to think about here than I ever imagined, and though much of it is really nice and warm and fuzzy, some of it is just plain scary. I've got to believe my husband understands this, that it's just a little overwhelming sometimes, and sometimes I just want to hide. I bet that deep down, he knows I don't want to run away.

I bet that deep down, they both do.

—⚬—

"HOP ON," MY NURSE SAID.

"Can't I use the other one?" I asked. "This scale always

makes me about 50 pounds heavier! Can't I use the one in the hall? Please?"

She tried not to glare at me because she likes me, but I knew she wanted to.

"There is no whining in this room. Get on the scale."

Pouting, I did as I was told, because I really respect this woman and didn't want to irritate her. That, and she had access to what I assume was an entire drawerful of needles. This being my third trimester, I'm pretty familiar with where they keep things...LIKE THE LIGHTER SCALE, I thought to myself, pouting some more.

And of course when I got on the scale, she had to keep sliding that blasted weight to the right and more to the right and more to the right until I finally had to point out that it had no place left to go. Apparently I had gained more than the allotted three pounds this month...according to that scale. Which, of course, was wrong.

She duly noted my chart and brought me to the examining room, somewhat pleased, I think, that she didn't have to hurt me, and closed the door.

Ah! But she didn't lock it! Her mistake! I stealthily slipped off the examining table (as "stealthily," say, as a beached whale making its way back to water, but you can't blame a girl for trying, OK?) and slowly, silently opened the door.

With "Mission: Impossible" music playing in the background (in Muzak, of course, but darn good timing nevertheless), I slipped out the door, ducked under the nurses' station to avoid detection, and scurried along the hallway in search of The Good

Scale. I was determined to correct this glaring error before the doctor had a chance to see the chart.

I had one close call when I heard my nurse's voice coming from another exam room. In retrospect I must have looked pretty silly flattening my back against the wall when my stomach reached clear to the other side, but I tingled with the danger of it anyway. Sad, but true.

When the coast was clear once again, I scurried around the corner and behold! There it was! The Good Scale! Justice was in sight as I approached it and carefully climbed aboard. When I was sure the needle had stopped moving, I opened my eyes...and almost fell off the darn thing. How could this be? The Good Scale had gone over to the dark side! I stood there, paralyzed, transfixed by the *exact same number* shown to me by the Demon Scale! It was a conspiracy. It had to be.

I stepped off and back on again. No change. I took off my socks. Nothing. I took off my watch. It didn't budge. I was about to take off my clothes when I heard the doctor's voice around the corner. I fled back to my room, heaved myself back on the examining table (which was neither easy nor pretty, I might add), and waited, defeated.

Afterwards I ran into another nurse friend.

"I don't understand it," I said. "I've done everything right. I take my vitamins, exercise, I've kept my keen sense of humor, and I'm still packing on the pounds. I just don't get it."

"There, there, now," she said, sympathetically. "Tootsie roll?"

"OK!" I cried happily. "Thanks!"

—⁂—

"DO YOU KNOW WHAT YOU'RE HAVING?" the salesman asked helpfully. "Sometimes that'll make your decision for you." I was looking somewhat doubtfully at a pink snowsuit, wondering how we reached the millennium without having addressed this color issue.

"It doesn't matter," I replied. "I don't like pink. I don't like it on girls, I don't like it on boys, I don't even like it on flamingos, where it actually belongs. Nor am I particularly fond of blue, come to think of it. And I may as well confess that yellow and mint green don't really do it for me either. I just want a teeny white snowsuit.

"Until this child can provide thoughtful feedback (with supporting arguments in a double-spaced brief) on the merits of pastels, then I believe the choice is mine, and I choose white. I don't understand why I can't find it. Are the color people afraid I'm going to drop the poor thing in the snow and lose it until spring?"

He skulked off, apparently deciding that he could not, in fact, help me. Well, that was certainly smooth, I thought. I'm completely lost in this unknown territory, and I just dissed the first person to offer guidance and support. Weeeeee! Good for me! On to the next department!

"Do you know what you're having?" chirped the irritatingly perky woman in bedding. "That will help you pick a theme for the nursery! We have Winnie the Pooh, Barbie, and of course all of the Disney characters!" There were about a zillion to choose from. This-is-the-fun-part, this-is-the-fun-part, I silently chanted.

"Do you have any plain animals?" I asked. "I like animals.

I watch the Discovery Channel. I'd like a blanket with animals on it. An elephant, a lion, maybe a bear. Normal animals, such as you'd find in the woods. Can we do that?"

"Well, of course," she stammered, "but, er, what if it's a girl?"

I was reminded of the Little League World Series announcer who said, "And next up is little Johnny Doe, whose *mother* is a dentist!" The emphasis was a dead giveaway that the guy was over 90, and so I let it pass with merely a chuckle. This woman, however, was younger than me. A chuckle was not going to make me feel better.

"Oh my God," I cried. "You're right! What was I *thinking*? Imagine — a girl surrounded by such masculine images! What a moron I am! We certainly wouldn't want her to grow up to be a — *gasp* — vet!"

And off she went. I was beginning to notice a distinct scarcity of fresh salespeople. Jeez, I thought — talk about no sense of humor! This is how I handle stress! Come back!

There was, thankfully, a nice young man who told me about breast pumps and the advantages of nursing and the paraphernalia involved. I admit I was somewhat uncomfortable discussing such an intimate part of my anatomy with him, until his complete disinterest in me as a woman convinced me that it stopped being an intimate part the day I got pregnant. But then, total strangers rub my stomach. I should realize that intimacy isn't what it used to be.

I am realizing, finally, that nothing will be again. This really is just the beginning — the car seat, stroller, crib, bassinet, diapers, little tiny bathtubs and washcloths and booties and those one-piece things with the snaps...but what a blast it's been so far. It's a whole new world, one that I am, at last, unbelievably thrilled to be invited into.

And every time I get frustrated or scared, I just stop for a few minutes and feel this little thing squirming and dancing and playing with its feet and kicking me for leaning too close to the sink. And I laughingly remember what everyone asks — "Do you know what you're having?"

Of course I do. I'm having a baby.

—∽—

IF THERE IS ONE THING I KNOW about childbirth, it's this: It will happen. Somehow. If you're pregnant and due, the baby will come out. It's a physical impossibility to be pregnant with the same child for the rest of your life.

Of course, if you're having a normal pregnancy, you don't know *when* it will come. That's not up to you. You can't will it out. You can't bargain with it. You can't reason with it. You can't bribe it. It will come out eventually, when it's ready. This is what I know.

Unfortunately I tend to forget it when faced with the inevitable inquiry, "Haven't you had that baby yet?" It's a harmless enough question to the average Joe, but to the nine-months-pregnant woman it comes out as, "What the heck's the matter with you? What are you doing wrong? Have that baby, for Pete's sake!"

It's almost as painful as hearing, "Did you have your baby yet?" a month after giving birth. Almost. Not quite.

Anyhoo, if I were to do this again, I'd probably ask the doctor to lie about my due date, even to me. I would ask her to say that it's actually past when it really is, and then even if I went late, everyone — including me — would still believe I was early. End of dilemma.

Why does the last month seem so long? It's as if time... simply...stops. By this point I've almost completely lost sight of the miracle at the end of the tunnel. My last appointment went something like this: "I don't care if I'm only 37 weeks. I'm 170 pounds. Induce me."

Ah, well. It's pregnant women like me who give pregnant women everywhere a bad rep, I know. And I know that people ask us The Question out of concern, and of course we're grateful.

I also know, however, that I'm very hormonal with way too much time on my hands this week, and have therefore taken the liberty of providing some possible responses to the inevitable inquiry for future generations of pregnant women everywhere. The question, of course, is "Are you still here?"

- "Yes, and apparently so are you. Now what can we do about that?"

- "Well, there's a funny story there. Turns out I'm not really pregnant after all. I just wanted to see what it was like to weigh more than my husband."

- "You know how it is. The baby and I are still bonding...apparently with some sort of permanent adhesive."

- "No, I'm a figment of your imagination. Weeeeee! Look at me! I'm a pink elephant!"

- "Yes. And you're still irritating. The difference is, some-day I'm going to give birth."

∾ "No, actually you've reached my answering machine. Please leave a message after I — er, *the* — beep."

∾ "Rumor has it the baby's heard about my culinary prowess. It's hiding."

It's ironic, really, because I have such mixed emotions about the whole thing. Sometimes I lie in bed thinking, Please let me go into labor. Please let me go into labor. Please let me go into labor. I want to see the baby, and to get on with life.

Then there was a moment a couple weeks ago when I thought I was in labor and all I could think was, no. No. No. No. No. Not today. No. No. Please. No.

So I guess I know two things about childbirth. First, I know it'll happen. And second, whenever it does…I know I won't be ready.

—∽—

I THINK IT'S TIME TO INTRODUCE YOU to my son. And from all of his squirming and chatting and fussing, I get the distinct impression he's ready to meet you. Or he has gas. Sometimes I can't tell.

Regardless, before we make these elaborate introductions, I'd like to make a few simple observations about the whole "baby" experience, now that I've actually had it. So pull up a bouncy seat and gather 'round, kids. Mommy Maggie has the floor.

I will begin by confessing that he is so absolutely beautiful, I spend most waking moments just trying to memorize his face. He has this clear-eyed, innocent look which leads me to suspect that I will deny him nothing. It leads me, as well, to the inescapable conclusion that he was worth it.

Worth what, you ask? Well, that is certainly an interesting and worthwhile question; moms, maybe you can help me out here. How's this: He was worth nine months of body-damaging pregnancy, constant worry about his health, and the mental trauma associated with a complete lifestyle change — oh, and THE MOST EXCRUCIATING PAIN I HAVE EVER ENDURED.

That about sum it up, d'ya think?

Yep, suffice it to say that calling it "labor" is like saying the Sistine Chapel has "pretty pictures." I still can't believe people experience that kind of pain and live. Either my threshold is somewhat lower than I had anticipated, or women who know are afraid the truth would result in the end of the world — which, incidentally, it would. Must be that post-natal amnesia syndrome, which I personally don't envision happening absent a blow to the head.

Besides, I don't want to forget, not any of it. Not the nurse who attached my hospital bracelet, to whom I offered my home to plunge her scissors into my chest, or the one who actually recorded the profanities I invented during contractions, or the first words I heard after the birth of my child, the doctor's consolation to my husband — "Don't worry; it'll go down," talking about his head. I'm assuming.

That said, how can I now explain the miracle of him? How can I describe his little button face, or how he purses his lips into a tiny Cheerio when he's thinking really hard? I simply can't, any more than I can convey the look on his face when we met for the first time. It either said, "Hey! Nice to meet you!" or "Egad! What's up with the hair?!" My response, I fear, lacked a similar passion. "Hi. OK, can I sleep now?"

But I've gotten better, I think. I mean, look what I've learned already! For instance, spit-up, sans obstacles, can actually travel several feet. "Leak-proof" diapers aren't. Poop, of the proper color and consistency, can actually be a source of joy and celebration. And sleep, contrary to popular belief, does not come naturally to all infants.

But then comes the magical day when you start to differentiate his "Hey, I'm starving here!" cry from his "Could you put a more stupid outfit on me?" cry. And he smiles his first real smile (read: "unaccompanied by gas"). And one day he's looking up at you and his head doesn't flop against your chest, and you realize your little man is growing up. Way too fast.

I don't know where this journey will take us from here, but I do know that I never again want to face life without this little person by my side. I'll always try to do the right things, but even when I make mistakes, he'll forgive me because he knows, somehow, that I love him more than life itself. And I know, somehow, that he loves me back.

So here he is. World, I give to you my son. And my son, I give to you...the world.

—⁓—

"WOULDN'T IT BE COOL if we knew what he was saying?" my husband said, as we listened to our son's babyspeak. "I mean, it's so obvious he's trying to tell us something — the facial movements, the expressiveness, the laughing — he's really talking!"

I have to admit it would be nice to know what he's trying

to say. We have doctors and books and friends and family to make sure we're doing all the right things — or not — and yet the one person who can really tell us if we're doing OK...can't. I think it'd be great, just once in a while, to hear our son say, "Hey, guys! Nice job!"

And while he may not speak five languages yet, as we may have erroneously suggested to our family, he's definitely on a verbal roll. It's no longer just the occasional coo or gurgle, either, no, sir. This kid is Chatty Cathy. He babbles on and on, with or without an audience. You gotta love someone who can carry on entire conversations with himself, don't you? Or worry about him, I guess.

At any rate, I've been thinking about this little situation so much that I unfortunately can no longer listen to him without imagining a cartoon cloud over his head containing the translation.

For instance, I was quietly watching him tell a whopper of a story to his hands. His face got solemn, he furrowed his little brow, he made all sorts of serious noises, and then burst out laughing, like he just cracked himself up. "Well, mister," I said perkily, sitting down beside him, "sounds like a good little story there. Would you like to share it with the rest of the class?"

He looked at me with a little irritation, I think, as though I interrupted him or something. "Gee, I would," said the bubble above his head, "if I thought 'the class' would get it."

Ouch. That hurt.

Then there was the dinner table last night, where our little guy enjoyed our riveting conversation. He sat there yawning, contemplating his lot and watching our actions, and when we were finished he gave us a beautiful smile which said, "How was that, huh? Did you enjoy it? Are you really, really full now? Good! Now come over here and let me beat you until you burp."

And of course there are those precious moments by the crib in the morning, when I try to ensure that he wakes up in a good mood by being incredibly happy myself. "How's my little baby this morning, hmmm?" I coo, "How's my little baby this morning?" And then that blasted bubble appears. "Hey, Mom, you know what? You don't have to say everything twice, OK? I'm a baby. I'm not an idiot."

Oh, and let's not forget the changing table, where we spend a good part of the day making sure my little angel is always clean and dry. Even these precious moments are now tainted by this little game I seem obsessed with playing. "Gee, Mom," I envision, "I appreciate your enthusiasm for what is truly a dirty job, but can I make a small suggestion? See those red lines around my stomach and thighs? Well, I'm just guessing here, but I think it means THE DIAPERS ARE TOO TIGHT."

And of course we can't forget Decker, can we? We've made sure the baby and dog have gotten to know and love each other just as we love them both. The cloud? Yep, it's there, every time I let them spend time together. "Yes, yes, I love the dog. Now, would you be a dear and get the hair out of my mouth?"

I believe my husband is right. This baby is definitely trying to tell us something with all of his chattering and weird-baby-noise-making. The difference between us, though, is that...

I don't want to know what it is.

—⁓—

"HONEY," MY HUSBAND SAID GENTLY, "I think it's time to call somebody. I think we need some help."

"*What*?" I was stunned. "What are you talking about? We're doing just fine. Really! I think we're fine!"

"I know we're fine," he said, "but I think things could be better. Come on — I know you know what I'm talking about. I know you've noticed it. I know it bothers you just as much as it bothers me."

"But...but..." I was blubbering. "I'll do better, I promise. Please. Just give me another chance!"

"I'm not blaming you, Mag — I'm just saying it's time we got some help for it. That's all. No one's judging you here, especially me."

"Well, you shouldn't, because it's not just my fault, you know!" Time for a counterattack. "You try staying home with a toddler who doesn't stop moving for 14 hours and see how much energy you have!"

He sighed, obviously not impressed with my dramatic range of histrionics. "Maybe we should talk about this some other time."

"OK," I said, victorious. "How's never? Is never good for you?" I then walked away.

What's the big deal here, anyway? I never cared much about it in my younger days, could take it or leave it, actually. I just wasn't one of those girls. Heck, I could go weeks — months! — without giving it a thought. But when I met my husband, I guess it did become a little more important.

At first I just wanted to do it for him, to make him happy. But eventually I did it for me, too, because it made me happy. I liked it. It gave me a sense of accomplishment. Then, of course, along came the baby, and that changed everything. Just like everyone said it would.

Oh, sure, it was still just as important, and it was still pretty easy when he was smaller. But the older he gets, the more difficult it gets. We either don't have the time, or don't make the time, or I'm too tired, or he's too tired, but whatever the reason, it's just not getting done.

But get help? Bring a stranger into our little world, expose ourselves in all our shame? I don't think so. The fact that I carry a Tigger key chain does not mean I have no pride.

And how could I explain the problem, particularly if this outsider has no children? The hours upon hours of playing, the toys, the clothes on the floor, the plethora of meals and snacks…how could I ever convey the profound sense of weariness and frustration at the end of each day as I decide, again, that it's easier to just sleep?

Maybe I'm just lazy. In fact, I'm reasonably certain it's a good possibility. And let's not forget that before my husband arrived on the scene, I couldn't care less about this sort of thing. Maybe I just have to accept the possibility that I regressed somehow. I went to break the bad news to my husband.

"But don't you remember the good old days?" he cajoled. "Remember how it used to be? The kitchen…the bathroom… the floor of the…"

"All right!" I cried. "Stop! Enough already! You win! You're right! We have a problem! Do what you have to do!"

I stormed out of the room as he dialed the phone. Well, I

thought, it's out of my hands. And it's for the good of the entire family. Of course I wish it hadn't come to this, but it had.

"Hello?" he said. "Acme Housecleaning?"

—⚬—

SOME THINGS NEVER CHANGE, I thought to myself as I lounged in the bathtub, still the only truly peaceful place in my world. Slowly, however, my gaze was drawn to a little yellow rubber duck, so composed and tranquil in the corner of the tub once reserved for my musk-scented body wash.

(Sigh.) I guess some things do.

Everyone said this would happen when we had a baby. They said it when we got married, too, that things wouldn't be the same between us. And the funny thing is, I always got the impression that they said it like it was a bad thing, like they were trying to scare us. Big bullies.

Sure, things have changed. And maybe at the beginning it didn't seem that it was necessarily for the better, as I recall the night my mother baby-sat so we could go out to dinner. If I remember correctly, we spent the evening, um, "discussing" child-rearing techniques and whether to have another baby. And by dessert we weren't discussing anything at all.

Lesson learned: If your memory of having a baby still prompts you to curl up in a fetal position and scream for drugs, you're probably not ready to discuss having another one.

But we were just getting used to the little guy, so that one doesn't count. What counts are all the other changes, the ones that people don't talk about, the ones that occur when you trust someone so deeply that there's nothing left to hide. And let's face it — after you've experienced childbirth together, there's nothing left to hide.

For example, I've discovered that my husband likes to cook. Well, actually, I think he likes to eat, and I don't always have time to cook. Whatever. But he's doing it, and he's pretty good at it, too, if he does say so himself. Which he does.

Yep, Chef Raphael has entered the building. He even has his own hot sauce collection, stored on a custom-made Wall of Flame to which he occasionally invites spectators. I told him he should start his own band, the Spice Boys, and he could be "Old Spice." Either he wasn't amused, or he didn't get it. I'm not sure.

And me? Well, it turns out that I'm somewhat of a nurturer after all. This was one of my bigger fears when I was pregnant, that when my baby cried my instinctive response would be, "Get over it." I was concerned that I wouldn't have the patience to care for an infant, and I was reasonably sure I'd have a problem with nighttime feedings.

Even my husband was a little nervous. When people set you up on a blind date, you know how you're generally in trouble when the description involves the words "nice personality"? Well, people would ask him how he thought I'd be as a mom, and his response was, "Um, she has a nice personality."

But I think I'm doing OK. I change a mean diaper, I no longer stub my hip on the corner of the bed in the middle of the night, I'm learning the little songs, and I would drop everything if my son needed me — except, obviously, my son. AND I've got a nice personality.

And what's all the brouhaha about loss of romance after

having a baby? So our definition of "passionate" is now "both awake." So our main topic of conversation is poop. So our previously spontaneous afternoon outings now involve packing a small suitcase. So what. I don't care what they say. The most romantic thing I've ever seen in my life is watching my husband with his son.

Sure, I might miss my sensuous body wash from time to time, but if I had it to do all over again...well, what can I say?

Rubber ducky, you're the one, you make bath time...

—⁓—

"HONEY, HAVE YOU CHANGED any poopy diapers today?" I asked.

"No, why? Hasn't he gone yet?" my husband answered.

"Nope. Don't think so."

"Hmm."

(Sigh.) You know you're married when, huh?

But that's not really a fair assessment. I mean, it's certainly not that my husband and I have nothing left to say to each other. It's just that if conversation is really an art, then what used to be a Picasso has taken on more of a hotel-room quality these days. But darn it, hotel room paintings are underrated.

Oh, sure, the witty repartee was generously sprinkled throughout our early years. It was easier then. How could it not be? New relationships hold tremendous mystery and surprise. He doesn't know you, and you don't know him, and so absolutely everything about each other is new. New and, therefore, exciting.

It takes weeks, months, even years to get to know one

another. You share all sorts of information and history about yourself, and he shares all sorts of stuff with you, and neither of you even stops to question the fact that all of these stories are essentially uncorroborated. Hey, you're in love.

You tell each other about work and school and growing up and past relationships and goals and dreams and fears. You take trips and go out to dinner and see movies, and all of these things inspire more anecdotes and cute little vignettes of your life that cannot be verified without an awful lot of digging.

And then you get married and have a baby and go visit your brother and you say, "Hey, Joe, remember the time we were fishing and I accidentally pierced your ear with a fish hook?" and he says, "You didn't do that. I did that. I don't even think you were there," and you say, "No — really? Hahaha...oops," and suddenly you realize that there's a very slim possibility that you may have, unintentionally, of course, exaggerated a story or two over the years.

You don't do it to be cruel or misleading; you just, in your mind and therefore in your conversation, make things a little more exciting than they might actually have been. You want to impress this other person. It's perfectly natural. Of course, it's probably not as natural to start believing the embellishments as truth, but we'll leave that one to the professionals.

At any rate, I think what happens is that once you hook up with someone for an extended period of time, you pretty much have to lose the embellishment angle because the truth is way too obvious. The other person's *there*. Even the most talented among us would be hard pressed to put an exciting spin on an event that our spouse actually witnessed.

For instance, if I said, "Hey, honey, our infant son spoke a complete sentence today — in Spanish!" he'd know right off the bat that I was exaggerating. I mean, everyone knows the baby's taking French as his second language — doh! There I go again!

And I thought "making an honest woman out of me" was about virtue. Silly me.

The good news is, we're not at the "So how 'bout them Bills?" stage. We both happen to find our lives quite exciting right now, and we're making a concerted effort to ensure that our conversation reflects that excitement, the way it did when everything about each other was new and, it turns out, inflated. Hey, we're dealing with reality now, and if you don't think reality's a hoot, then you haven't been to our house lately.

"Honey, you won't *believe* this diaper! I *mean* it! You *have* to see this!"

—⁓—

O, Heather, Where Art Thou?

I WAS WAITING NERVOUSLY, wondering what demonic hormonal imbalance had forced me into such drastic measures. Finally my savior came in the room.

"Hello!" she said brightly. "You must be Maggie! What brings you here today?"

"I need a change," I replied, trembling. "I'm heading toward 50."

She looked confused as she asked, "And you're here to...?"

"Look 20," I said.

The confused look remained.

"Thirty, then," I pleaded. "All right! Forty! I can live with 40!"

She continued to just kind of stare at me. I looked around to make sure I was in the right place.

"You do faces, right? Well, I want to look like this," I said, thrusting a picture towards her. The confused look turned to something resembling fright.

"That's Heather Locklear," she said.

"I know, and look at her!" I cried. "She's my age! Isn't she gorgeous? That's how I want to look!"

"I can't make you look like Heather Locklear!" she exclaimed.

"Oh, come on!" I demanded. "This is the 21ˢᵗ century! The new millennium, for crying out loud! Just sandblast the whole thing and put some cream on it! How hard can it be? You can clone a herd of sheep but you can't make me look like Heather?" I was bordering on hysterical.

"I'll tell you what, sweetie," she said, "you just stay right here while I go and find a nice security guard…"

She was now giving me the same sad look I'd gotten from my husband earlier in the week, the look reserved for people who are clearly having a breakdown of some sort. The difference is that my husband knows me. He was more irritated than frightened.

"Honey," I started, gently, "I'm having a midlife crisis. I need a few changes. I want to start taking care of my skin, and I want to join a gym. I need new clothes and new glasses. I want to look like I did before kids. Oh, and one more thing," I continued, "I might need to start flirting with the UPS man."

"You can't be having a midlife crisis!" he said. "You just grew up last year! You have a kid in diapers!"

"Well, I hardly see how that matters," I retorted. "So I had a protracted childhood and got a late start in the baby thing. It's called 'midlife crisis,' not 'mid-adulthood crisis.' Having young kids never stopped *men* from clinging to youth, did it?"

"I didn't have a midlife crisis," he said, "and I'm older than you."

"You know why?" I shot back. "Young women look at you

and think 'Mel Gibson.' Young men look at me and think 'the mom on Happy Days.' Men age better than women. It's one of life's great mysteries — although I myself blame childbirth."

"OK," he responded, after some thought. "Let's start with the face and the gym. You can buy some new clothes. Get your glasses. Maybe then we'll revisit the flirting issue." He walked away, shaking his head.

So that's how I ended up at the salon. I just wanted the nice young woman to put something on my face to undo the sun damage and age damage and what-do-you-*mean*-you-don't-use-moisturizer damage. I didn't even care if it hurt, I told her; heck, I've given birth without an epidural! Bring it on!

"OK," she replied, "let me explain. This is a facial. We remove old, tired skin to uncover the newer skin beneath. Do you understand? It's new skin. It's not a new face. You're still going to look like you."

"Well, I was hoping for something a little more dramatic," I said. "But I guess you can only work with what you've got." Suddenly inspiration struck as I glanced longingly at my picture of Heather.

"Hey," I asked brightly, "do you do hair?"

—〰—

STANDING IN LINE AT THE GROCERY STORE the other day, I couldn't help skimming the covers of the various women's magazines. They all seemed to focus on how to get a man and how to impress a man and how to please a man and how to tell if your man is worth the time of day. And they all assumed I was single.

I was suddenly reminded of a conversation between my husband and I that took place about a month after we were married. The conversation involved a revelation I'd just had, to the effect that we were no longer allowed to date other people. It kind of bummed me out because, frankly, I enjoyed dating.

Well, hey — what about me? I wondered, returning to the present. Should I no longer be interested in the finer points of romance simply because my dating pool has narrowed somewhat? And while I'm at it, shouldn't they be asking people like *me* for the dating tips? I mean, if I'm married, then presumably I did something right, right?

It's not fair, really. I like a nice restaurant as much as the next girl, but apparently I no longer rate. Maybe this is why marriages suffer from time to time, because we let the romance and excitement kind of drift away. And why does this happen?

Because nobody offers us dating tips, that's why.

Well, that's all going to change right now. I'm not quite ready to throw in the excitement towel. A friend and his wife have been married over 25 years and they told me they still date every Saturday night. True story. Of course, I'm assuming they meant each other...I mean, I never thought to ask...

At any rate, I believe you can be married — and have kids, for that matter — and still maintain the romance of your dating days. Well, "maintain" may be too strong a word here; how about "revisit"? Does that do it? Works for me. And I'm convinced that if I can just follow my own advice, my husband will ask me out.

Let's start with the basics. If you're a stay-at-home mom, what's the first thing that springs to mind when you think of romancing your husband? Yes! Brushing your teeth. And your hair. Hey, if you can squeeze in a shower, you go, girl. Otherwise, just try to be clean. I'm not saying it will work for everyone, but...

If you're out in the work world, you've got a leg up, so to speak. You're already dressed when dinnertime rolls around. And there's probably no spit-up on your shirt. All you have to say is, "Gee, honey, see how nice I look? I think we should go out to dinner!" If the fact that you look nice five days a week escapes him, then you're good to go!

And men, you've got to participate. We know you work hard all day, but you know what? So do we. Suck it up. And relax a little bit already! Dating your wife shouldn't be stressful; it's not like you're worrying all night about whether to kiss her. Just do what you did in the old days — and after you've both had a good laugh, take her out!

Of course, there are other, more subtle ways to flirt with each other and keep the sparks alive. Flowers are good. Emptying the garbage works. An impromptu peck on the cheek can do miracles. And my husband is always thrilled when I ask him to change a diaper that's merely wet. Gives him chills, it does.

And that, from what I remember, is what romance is all about.

—∞—

"DARN IT!" MY MOM SAID AS WE CHATTED on the phone. "I'm watering this plant and it's going right through! There's water all over the place! What the heck is wrong with it?

"Oh, wait a minute," she continued after a moment, "I see the problem. The soil isn't wet at all. I don't have my glasses on, and it seems I missed the plant altogether...(sigh)...oh, well. Needed to wash that windowsill anyway!"

My mom has this way of making everything seem OK. Whatever life throws at her, she makes the best of it. I am *so* not like her. I live in what is apparently a constant state of denial. It may even be a country. When I see the signs of aging, I manage to attribute them to something more acceptable, like alien takeover. It's a gift, really.

But the intellectual side of me (which, granted, can only be seen with an electron microscope) cannot deny the truth. Oh, sure, I'm not borrowing my mom's pastel-print snap-front housecoat yet, but instead of the more traditional reaction of "Egads, Mom...nice sheet," I now silently appraise it with, "Boy, that sure looks comfortable."

So maybe it's time to admit that my body didn't stop plodding along the timeline of life when my mind did, which was, I believe, about 20 years ago. Maybe it's time to accept my maturing self with the dignity and grace expected of my age group. Then again, maybe not. Hey, a little denial never hurt de-no one, that's what I always say.

The main weapon in the "I'm not old just because I remember eight-tracks" arsenal is perception. "Old" used to mean anyone over 30. When I hit 30, it meant over 60. Now it's 120. I will accept I'm in the presence of someone old if her father fought in the Civil War.

Of course, there are more concrete signs that one's body has, er, "peaked." For example, a friend recently cried with delight, "Look! She has old lady arms just like the rest of us!"

This would be a concrete sign. And if I ever wear a sleeveless top again in my life, you may feel free to observe this phenomenon.

Want more? OK. Happy to oblige. You know your body is fading as fast as your mind when...

- You show pictures of your child to a colleague who says, "Your grandson is beautiful!"

- Salt and pepper are no longer a spice combination. They're a hair color.

- Phrases such as "more of me to love" and "home again, home again, jiggedy jig" pop into your head with frightening regularity.

- You have used "sensible" and "shoes" in the same sentence.

- Hot baths are no longer a luxury, unless you consider it a luxury to be able to stand up straight.

- You wake up one day to find a *Reader's Digest* on the back of your toilet...and read it.

- 10 p.m. has gone from "Woohoo! Party time!" to "Woohoo! Bed time!"

- The "locate handset" button on your telephone beats out the remote in order of importance.

- Clothes don't have to be fashionable. They just have to be loose.

- You no longer ask someone to repeat something so you have more time to come up with a snappy response. You ask him to repeat it because you didn't hear him.

And, of course, I share my mother's eyesight dilemma, which

was probably the most difficult to admit. But I thought my latest snafu would make her feel better.

"Well, Mom," I said cheerily, "just wanted you to know that I forgot to wear my glasses while changing a diaper...the poor dog's *still* plucking tape from his tail."

—∞—

"I'VE JUST GOT ONE QUESTION FOR EVERYONE," my sister-in-law cheerfully asked on the first night of our visit. "What'll it be for dinner?"

"Pizza!" her kids cried in unison.

"Pizza's great," my husband said. "Our treat!"

She looked at us with a somewhat confused expression, until understanding dawned and she remembered with whom she was dealing.

"Oh, that's OK," she said, almost apologetically, "I'll just whip one up. Won't take a second."

And she did. She threw together some ingredients I couldn't name if you paid me, used her fingers to shape it into a perfect circle, produced some sauce and cheese and pepperoni which she apparently just had on hand, if you can believe that, and voila! It was done. Homemade pizza — two words which, in my life, have never been used in the same sentence.

My husband and I were impressed. "Awestruck" might even work here. And that was just the beginning.

When dessert time came, she pulled out some ice cream (Ha! I thought to myself. Store-bought!), spooned it into dishes and said, "Who would like whipped cream?" All hands shot up, and she walked to the refrigerator to get what I supposed was the Cool Whip. But no-o-o-o-o. This woman, who obviously mentored Martha Stewart at some early point in her career, pulled out the heavy cream and sugar.

I had to do something.

"Hey, Aly," I said, "do me a favor, huh? Relax. You don't have to do all this. You married my brother, remember? As far as I'm concerned, that fulfilled your 'impress the family' obligation."

She laughed. "Wait until Renny starts eating real food. You'll be doing all of this too. I guarantee it." I looked at my son, this little guy I love more than life itself and for whom I would do just about anything, and thought, mmmmmmm, no. Don't think so.

I spent the rest of the trip watching her boil eggs for sandwiches and make salads from 19 different kinds of lettuce and slice almonds for desserts and whip up pancakes and waffles from scratch. My husband said I was napping when she baked bread. He started looking at me with what can only be described as growing disdain.

"Hey!" I shouted from the nearest rooftop. "I make a darn good glass of iced tea!" Total strangers came out of their homes and replied, in chorus, "It's from a can!"

Things went from bad to worse when we returned from the trip and took the baby for his nine-month check-up. His doctor advised that he was now ready for table food, three meals a day. It's no trouble, she said; just mash up some of whatever you're having and he should be able to handle it. The blank look on my face prompted the inquiry, "You do eat properly, don't you?"

My husband piped up, "I can field this one! My wife thinks 'balanced diet' means being able to hold a donut and a cup of coffee at the same —"

"Excuse me," I cut him off. "I'm capable of answering for myself. You were helpful, though. Now get out." I turned to the doctor. "I'm sure it will be easy enough to start eating correctly, especially if it's what my son needs."

Visions of the piles of baby food jars inhabiting our pantry floated through my mind. I couldn't bear to admit that I'd even incorporated them into my own diet. "I guess I just thought he'd be on baby food a little longer," I said. Until kindergarten, for instance.

That night was my very first test. The cupboard doors were wide open as I appraised my options, and after a good deal of struggling, I finally decided.

"I just have one question for you boys," I said brightly. "What's it going to be for dinner — takeout or delivery?"

—⁂—

YOU CAN'T TEACH AN OLD DOG new tricks, huh? Well, last night our dog came upstairs, woke me up as if he had to go to the bathroom, got me downstairs and, instead of heading toward the door, led me straight to his favorite sleeping spot, whereupon lay an errant blanket. He got me out of bed in the middle of the night to clear his cushion.

That would fall under "new trick" as far as I'm concerned.

So now that the new guy in my life is approaching the first birthday milestone, I'm wondering if I've been able to keep up with his learning curve, being the age I am. I'm not saying

I'm old, necessarily, but I do remember eight-track tapes, gauchos and feathered hair. So does that mean I'm no longer going to learn anything? Don't those sayings become sayings because they're true?

If that's the case, then logically we must reach a point when we say to ourselves, "Hey, I know pretty much everything I need to know, so I'm just going to take it easy for the next, er, forever." And compared to what my child's learned this year, I must be looking pre-e-tt-y rested.

Let's just look at the basics for a moment. This kid, in the space of one year, has learned to roll over, sit up, clap, crawl, pick up tiny things with his chubby little fingers, stand, walk, run, and scale a baby gate. Mommy, conversely, learned to make egg salad. Hmmm. I know that, on the surface, this doesn't look good.

But aside from those paltry accomplishments, I believe I've actually matched his learning curve. In fact, for every new thing he learns, I *have* to learn something, sort of like that "action-reaction" theory I vaguely remember reading something about at some point in my life...hey, give me a break, OK? I'm trying to keep up with an infant. I'm not applying to NASA.

At any rate, if you look at the year as a whole, I think you'll find that we can *so* learn new things even if the words "all skate, change directions" mean something to us.

For instance, the baby learned what seems like a zillion new words, including just about any word that begins with "d" as well as some more complicated phrases such as "What restaurant tonight, Mommy?" Of course, he was starting with nothing. He had no place to go but up.

Mommy, on the other hand, didn't learn any new words, because she already knew quite a few. She did, however, expand her repertoire of definitions. "Projectile," turns out, has several.

Baby learned that sleeping is a highly overrated and not visibly useful state. Mommy learned that coherency is a highly overrated and not visibly useful state.

Baby learned a variety of new food textures, tastes, colors and consistencies. Mommy learned that paper towels are cheaper in bulk.

Baby learned that when he starts crying, Mommy can usually make things better. Mommy learned that when *she* starts crying, her mommy can usually make things better.

Then, of course, there's the dog, who, in addition to acquiring the "mommy, fetch" skill, evidently memorized the Charlie Brown/Lucy/football scene. Our dear little child toddles toward him doing the Frankenstein shuffle, and as soon as he reaches him, the dog darts out of range and baby does a face-plant on the carpet. (See "new trick," above.)

And if that's not enough to convince you, think about this: last year at this time I could barely change a diaper, and now I can do it while the child is actually being held up in the air as we're running through the airport to catch a flight — without spilling a drop. Can't teach an old dog new tricks, huh? I just have one thing to say about that.

Woof.

—❧—

OK, I ADMIT IT, I'M AS AGE-CONSCIOUS as the next woman. I had a hard time when I grew a beard. I was a little put out when

Social Security sent me a schedule of projected benefits. And I know when men look at me, they're no longer wondering if I'm single; they're wondering if I have a single daughter.

But I just saw a commercial for facial cream that really got my goat (oh...my...GOD. "Got my goat"? Aaagggghhh!) The cream was for the treatment of wrinkles. According to my handy Oxford, "treatment" means "something done in order to cure an illness or abnormality."

Gee, here's an interesting thought — would someone like to tell George Clooney that there is now a treatment for those lines on his face which make him one of the more gorgeous and well-paid men alive? Oh, that's right — silly me. He's a man. Those are "character lines."

Why is it, when they're right up there with gray hairs and spreading derrieres in terms of non-discriminatory signs of aging, that wrinkles are abnormal on women? If they're so bad, then why aren't there any men doing those cream commercials? Why do women perceive our aging selves so differently than our male counterparts?

Men's wrinkled faces are "craggy" and "rugged." Women's are "lined" and "worn." It makes it sound as though men get theirs through a lifetime of adventures, while ours come from being old and tired. Well, I'm not tired, darn it. And I've had an adventure or two in my life. Not in the recent past, perhaps, but I've had 'em. I'm not lying.

And I'm guilty myself. For example, my friends get facials and peels and use expensive creams, and they all look great. So I had a facial a few months ago because I am, in fact, a sheep, and the young woman asked me how I cared for my face. "Well, not too much!" I laughed, nervously. "There're too many freckles, and my lips are pretty thin…"

She looked at me blankly for a moment, and then said, "No. I mean, what is your facial care regimen?"

"Oh, right," I replied. When I told her my, er, "regimen," she said my skin was in very good shape considering I've never done anything right. She then sold me $200 worth of cleansers, ointments and gels, guaranteed to return my skin to its glowing, youthful appearance.

I tried the stuff for weeks and concluded there's only one true anti-wrinkle formula — youth. And that's where it belongs. Wrinkles are a sign that we've lived some life. My friends don't look great because they don't have any wrinkles; they look great because they *do* have them.

They're trophies of our most intense moments — the things that made us laugh, the things that made us cry. And, a little less dramatically, the things that made us squint. If I could go back, I'd probably wear my glasses more. I mean, there are laugh lines, and there are "I'm too vain to wear glasses" lines, you know what I'm saying?

Anyhoo, I just had another interesting thought (two in one day! Who says old age is scary?!) The big rage all these years is anything that's natural, 100 percent cotton, right? Diapers, undershirts, T-shirts, blue jeans — whatever it is, it is simply not cool unless it's got that "100 percent cotton" tag.

And what does natural, 100 percent cotton do? That's right. It wrinkles. Ha!

Society still puts out the image of the sexy, beautiful supermodel as the ideal. Well, I've got an insight to share: those women are HALF OUR AGE. We're never going to look like that again, if we ever did. And there's nothing wrong with that. I look in the mirror now, see those telltale lines around the eyes and think, wow. I've got character.

Tons of it.

———

WE WERE EATING DINNER THE OTHER NIGHT when the waitress commented on how well-behaved our child was in the restaurant.

"He should be," my husband said. "He's been eating in them since birth."

She looked at us curiously. "You mean he doesn't eat at home, ever?"

"Oh, sure he does," he explained. "As long as he wants toast."

She fled before I could chime in that he can have any kind of toast he wants. I thought that was important to add.

The truth is, my husband and I are not what you'd call gourmands. Well, we're half-gourmand; we love to eat. We just don't love to cook. Never have, never will. Neither of us. What I'll never understand is why he's forgiven for it and I'm not.

He doesn't hold it against me, of course. He's known from the start that I was somewhat challenged in the kitchen arena, and accepted it as part of my charm. He's just one of those guys who truly believe that men and women are not predestined to certain roles. I keep waiting for his spaceship to return and beam him up. So far, so good.

And it's kind of amusing, the fact that even in today's day and age, not all men believe that. Back in my single days;

my dates would come over, see the empty refrigerator and exclaim, "Wow! You weren't kidding! You really don't cook! Isn't that cute!"

But many of them held onto this fantasy that after we fell in love and settled down together, I would magically whip out a white apron and prepare a five-course spread for unexpected company. Well, guys, you can all rest easy now, because — surprise! — it didn't happen.

Here's what I think my downfall was: "The way to a man's heart is through his stomach." That was a challenge if I ever heard one. I was going to prove that either a) I didn't *need* a man's heart, or b) if I did need one, I could get it on brains and charm alone. Yes, I married late. Thank you for asking.

At any rate, it seemed a little easier to justify back then too. Now because I have a family, people seem to think, OK, enough's enough. Really, we mean it. Start cooking. Broil vegetables. Steam chicken. Do whatever it is people do in the kitchen. Joke's over.

In fact, I found myself making excuses as time went by, because even I became somewhat ashamed of my "problem." For example, when I got engaged, I couldn't cook because I was simply too busy, all that planning and everything. When we got married, it was just so much more romantic to eat out.

Then I got pregnant and I was too tired, and besides, it was summer and just too hot. When the baby came, there never seemed to be a good time to cook, what with changing diapers and feeding baby and blah blah blah. And besides, it was winter, so it was just too cold.

But I have to stop making excuses. First of all, I shouldn't have to, and second of all, I'm running out of them. I just don't cook. I don't enjoy it, and I'm not good at it. Trust me. Ask any of my victims. It's not a joke. As my husband admits, cooking is out for me — we either eat out, or we order out. And it's the same for him.

So I'm learning once again to accept this personality quirk, although there are times when it is still slightly embarrassing. We were invited to a cookout this weekend, and like any good guest, I heard my husband ask, "Great! What can we bring?" I held my breath awaiting the response.

"Fine!" he said into the phone. "Whole wheat it is! See you then!"

—∞—

OK, BOYS, IT'S TIME WE HAD a little meeting.

Let me start by saying I'm very pleased with how things are going so far. Overall, you've both adjusted quite well to being siblings.

Now that we have some time under our belt, however, I'd like to suggest a few guidelines that will be helpful in achieving my long-term goal, which, as you know, is sanity. I've arranged these new guidelines, or rules, if you will, into a handy refrigerator-door directory for your convenience.

Decker, you're first because, after all, you *were* first. And yours was probably the more difficult transition, going from top dog to underdog with very little say in the matter. You handled it with grace, finesse, and very few accidents, and I couldn't be prouder. But there are a few areas in which I probably wasn't very clear.

For instance, I understand that the baby commandeered your area of the family room, and I'm sorry. But the oriental rug in the living room is not a napkin. You have to find somewhere else to wipe your mouth after you eat. The back yard, say.

And though your tendency to pick up whatever's laying on the floor held a certain charm in the past, I must confess it's beginning to bug me. The baby's stuffed animals are not chew toys. The baby's blocks are not chew toys. The baby's dirty clothes are not chew toys. And the baby is not a chew toy.

Which leads me to you, Renny. Now, you know I love you more than life, and there isn't a lot that I won't let you do. But now that you're old enough to actually *do* stuff, I'm having to rethink my position. I can't, in good conscience, continue to allow you the sheer pleasure of destroying everything in your path.

The dog is not a chair. You cannot sit on him. He is not a pool patiently awaiting the perfect swan dive. He is not a trampoline, and he is not a bed. Hugs are acceptable, but putting your finger in his eye and asking "Dat?" is not.

I also regret to advise that the dog is not your own personal wastebasket. Your initially amusing habit of accidentally dropping your dinner over the high chair into his waiting mouth is no longer amusing. Nor, incidentally, is it accidental, a fact I'm sure you thought escaped me. It did not.

In that same vein, the dog's water bowl is not your sink. And those little brown round things in his food dish are his food. They are not Milk Duds.

And that little game of throwing your ball over the baby gate to Deck? Fini, buddy. It took me a few times to catch on, I admit, but I finally did and you, sir, are busted. You think because Mommy writes her grocery list on MagnaDoodle that she's got a few lights out upstairs, but think again. Stop me if I'm wrong, but I believe it goes something like this:

Baby gives ball to dog, dog comes around the corner to mommy, Mommy pries ball out of dog's mouth, washes it and gives it back to baby, who goes around the corner to give ball to dog. How am I doing so far?

At any rate, for a dog, Deck, you've been incredibly patient, and for that I am eternally grateful. And for a baby, Ren, you've been incredibly lucky, and for that I am even more so. But now that you're both getting older, you need to start understanding the rules, and as I said, feel free to refer to them on the refrigerator at any time.

Meeting adjourned. You may now go play. And please, don't drool on each other.

—w—

"SO HOW'S THE DISCIPLINE COMING?" our son's doctor asked. "Any problems yet? Tantrums? Head-banging?"

"No, of course not!" I said defensively, as if it were unheard of for a toddler to act up. "I mean, sure, he does this thing every once in a while where he straightens his entire body out like a board and screams, but I hardly think that qualifies as a tantrum..."

She looked at me as she must look at all of her mothers experiencing complete denial and asked, "So what's your secret? I'm sure he gets into everything, and climbs onto everything, and undoes everything you try to do — how do you handle him?"

"Oh, it's easy!" I replied. "You've heard of clinical psychologists and forensic psychologists? Well, I'm training to become a reverse psychologist! It's a skill I've always been quite partial to, but this time I think it's really working! I may have a valid theory for once!"

Thus began the journey to incoherence that usually accompanies our visits to the pediatrician (nothing like defending yourself to a professional to make you feel like a true novice, you know what I'm saying?)

"Every time he wants to do something I don't want him to do," I continued, "I just let him do it! See, if he thinks he's allowed to do it, he won't want to do it anymore! Isn't it beautiful!? It works like a charm!"

She shook her head, managed an "OK, good luck! See you next time!" and fled. What was left unsaid went something like this:

"Let me get this straight. When he wants to do or have something you want him to do or have, you let him do or have it. When he wants to do or have something you don't want him to do or have, you let him do or have it. So your method of discipline is based on what, then — a complete lack of 'no'?"

And maybe she has a point. I mean, it is just now beginning to occur to me that children may actually want to do certain things because they're fun, and not simply because they're not supposed to do them.

It's a little harder than I thought, this whole discipline thing. I now understand the meaning of the expression, "This is going to hurt me more than it's going to hurt you." It absolutely kills me to scold or punish my son...or I'm sure it will, when that day comes.

But I ask you, how you can say "No!" to the most beautiful thing you've ever seen, even if he *is* sticking his hand in the garbage? I ask you, how effective is the message if you're stifling a giggle each time you do it?

Besides, the child simply doesn't get it. Whether he's touching the oven ("Hot," he cautions, placing his entire palm on it), opening child-proof latches ("Dis?" he asks, innocently), or calling Idaho ("Hi! Hi! Hi!" he cries to his new friend), he does not understand why Mommy is jumping around screaming for him to stop.

And where can you give a time-out to a toddler that isn't simply another place to play? "I'll show you, little guy. You sit right here on this chair — no! Don't stand up! Don't sit sideways! Don't turn around! Don't peer through the railings like you're in jail! Stop that! This isn't a game! I mean it!"

But hey — don't you worry about us, no sir. Mommy's been working on it, and she's going to be the discipline queen. In fact, I'm feeling stronger every day, and I think it's beginning to show. Yep, when I say "jump," my kid says, "How high?"

And "How far?" and "How often?" and "Off what?"

—∽—

"JUST WAIT UNTIL IT'S YOUR TURN!" my mom would say, tearing through the house after my diaperless baby brother and singing the classically misquoted Creedence lyrics, "There's a bathroom on the right." I of course would be laughing at her and thinking, egads, woman. You have got to get out more.

Now, however, it *is* my turn. And suffice it to say that I'm no longer the one laughing.

Let me begin by saying that no, I am not crazy. I had no intention of initiating this little trauma with one child while giving birth to another. In fact, I was thinking middle school was probably a good target for the whole process. But he, apparently, had other plans.

"I go potty!" he said. We were standing at the sink brushing our teeth.

"What?" I asked, looking around to see if there was someone else in the room.

"I go potty!" he said again. He got down from his little stepstool and stood adamantly before the toilet.

"Well, OK, little guy," I replied, hesitantly, "I mean, sure, if that's what you want to do..."

I certainly couldn't discourage him without being the focus of therapy for years to come. And besides, what kind of mother says, "No, honey, I'd really rather you stayed in diapers until you're old enough to date"? I dutifully took off his diaper and pants, popped in his little potty seat, and lifted him up.

"All done!" he squealed with delight.

"*What?*" I practically screamed. "What do you mean, all done? You haven't been up there 10 seconds!"

"All done!" he said again, and started to hop down. He stood there in the middle of the bathroom, looking very proud of himself, and proceeded to pee on the floor. OK, I said to myself. It's just going to take some time.

"Good job, honey! Nice try! We'll get 'em next time!" I

said cheerfully. I then put a clean diaper on him, put his pants back on, cleaned up the floor, and started down the stairs.

"I go potty!" he called after me. "I go potty again!"

I stopped, somewhat less patient but knowing there was only one right thing to do. I turned around and headed back up the stairs into the bathroom, and started the process again. And again he cried, "All done!" after 10 seconds.

I then picked him up and carried him downstairs, crying because Mean Mommy wouldn't let him jump on and off the potty for the next four hours, and said, "OK, Daddy, your turn!"

My husband took him upstairs and put him on the potty, where he proceeded to do his business as if he'd been doing it for 30 years. I heard the cheering and celebrating and high fives, thought of all the times my husband opened a jar I'd struggled with, and muttered, "Yeah, well, I loosened the cap."

And of course it is a big deal. He called both grandmas to share the news —"Hi grandma! I go potty! I go pee pee and poopy!" — and they were appropriately excited. The cashier at the supermarket, of course, lacked the family connection, and so her enthusiasm was somewhat subdued.

"I go potty!" he cried at the checkout.

"You did?" she said. "How exciting!"

"I go pee pee and poopy!" he said, beaming.

"Well, that's just...lovely..." she trailed off, turning green.

But that's OK. I know not everyone understands. Heck, there are days when I'm still not as enthusiastic as I should be, although I try my best to keep a sense of humor about it. In fact, every time I find myself chasing a diaperless toddler through the house, I sing just like my mom used to, although I choose to misquote another classic.

"It's my potty and I'll cry if I want to…"

—⁓—

Old Dogs, New Tricks

WHEN I WAS PREGNANT THE FIRST TIME, I couldn't stand that knowing look I'd get from women who'd already gone through what I was about to go through. They looked at me with a mixture of pity, sympathy, and a sort of disdain that I couldn't quite fathom.

When they asked, "Is it your first?" it wasn't because they cared whether it was my first. They were wondering if I had a clue yet, which would allow them to truly dialogue with me about children instead of nodding their heads and saying politely, "That's nice, dear," and walking away.

Of course I didn't let it bother me, but I distinctly remember pouting a little after such conversations and thinking, "Jeesh. What's the matter with *her*?" I would then waddle away, hand dramatically on belly, and look for a good place to nap.

As I think back on that time of my life and compare it with this pregnancy, it occurs to me that only one conclusion can be drawn. I had way too much time on my hands back then.

I'd never begrudge me that naïve and wondrous time — nor did these other women — but I now understand from where that subsequent knowing look comes. It comes, in a word, from knowing. It's like that popular mommy definition of "sterilizing" — what you do to your first baby's pacifier by boiling it and your last by blowing on it.

It's what you can only learn along the way...not that I necessarily condone blowing on a pacifier. But sometimes there's just no sink, OK?

And the differences start long before the second child is born. For instance, my first pregnancy felt like it lasted three years. This time it seems like delivery is right around the corner...which, actually, it is. Yikes.

Along those same lines, at any given time during my first pregnancy, I had no problem answering the "How far along?" question. It usually went something like this: "Well, let's see...28 weeks, four days, nine hours, and — do you have a watch? — OK, 12 minutes."

This time I'm not quite as conscious of that issue. I'm due in November. That's what I know.

The first time, my passing nausea was a source of great turmoil and concern. Now it's, "Yeah, I'm having some vomiting this time — no big deal. Hey, can I use that baggie?"

The first time I gained 65 pounds because, in retrospect, all I did was eat and sleep. This time I've put together words I can honestly say have never left my mouth before: "Am I gaining enough weight?" My doctor is getting pretty good at hiding his eye-rolling.

The first time I was afraid to carry a laundry basket, which didn't please my husband immensely. You can imagine his amusement, then, when I came in the house yesterday carrying a toddler, my purse (which any mom knows weighs 10 pounds), and a bag of groceries that included a gallon each of milk and orange juice.

My first child was treated to classical and symphony arrangements through state-of-the-art headphones strategically placed on Mommy's burgeoning tummy. My second child may or may not actually hear the Barney CDs playing in the background while I do housework.

And I'm sure things will be a little different when the baby arrives, not because I will care less, but because I will know more — things like the fact that plastic grocery bags are just as easy to use for diaper disposal as those cute-looking little pails that sell for 30 bucks.

And I guess, because I'm just that kind of girl, that the next time I meet someone who's pregnant for the first time, I'll be sincerely enthusiastic...and turn my head away before I smile knowingly.

—∿—

WHAT'S SO HARD ABOUT the terrible twos, anyway?

I mean, what's the big deal? My son Renny is starting to find his little personality. Good for him, I say. Now, infancy — that's another story. That's the hard phase, if you ask me. Take my little Sophie, for instance.

"Hello, baby girl! How's my little darlin' this morning? How's my good girl? Are you sleepy again? That's OK, honey... just take another little rest."

Anyway, as I was saying, babies eat, they cry, then they eat some more, all day long . . just like Mommy, come to think of it. It's taxing, I tell you.

Toddlers, God bless 'em, can walk and talk and do a lot of things for themselves. So really, how hard can it —

"Renny, please stop running. I mean it. Slow down."

Sorry. As I was saying, how hard can it be? Infants can't do anything, so their dependency is complete. My son, on the other hand, is his own man.

"Renny, please put that down. That's Mommy's cup. Hot, hot, hot. Put it down. Please put it down. NOW."

So where was I? Oh, yes. My son barely needs me anymore. He's old enough to eat by himself, and he's learning how to put his own clothes on -

"Where are your pants? Please put them back on. It's cold. We're not going to the store until you put your pants back on. I'm serious. Put them back on. Do you want to go to the store, or do you want to stay home? Fine. You can stay home.

"No, you can't stay home. Where are your pants? Come on, honey. Help Mommy here. Please get dressed. And *please stop running.*"

And infants can't really amuse themselves, you know what I'm saying? You have to entertain them. Not so with my little guy. He entertains himself.

"Do not use that crayon on the wall! That's why we have paper! STOP WRITING ON THE WALL! And *please* do not run with the crayon in your mouth!"

Of course, the dog enjoys my son more now that he's bigger. He has a playmate now, and I think he's really learning to like him.

"Don't throw that at the dog. No, honey — that's not what Mommy meant. I meant, don't throw *anything* at the dog. And *please* stop running. Please."

Oh, sure, he can't change his own diaper yet, but the potty training's coming right along, and I'm sure he only regressed because of the new baby. Besides, it's a little ritual we have, he and I, and neither of us are in a hurry to give it up.

"Renny, hold still. I have to change your diaper. Hold still. You didn't want to use the potty so hold still. *Hold still.* HOLD STILL!"

But that aside, my guy is wonderful. He likes nothing better than to please Mommy. He's my little helper, he is.

"Time to put your toys away, honey. Nap time. Clean up, clean up, everybody everywhere...no, don't take those blocks out. We're cleaning up now. Please don't take those blocks out. Put your cars away. DON'T TAKE THOSE BLOCKS OUT.

"And please STOP RUNNING! That's the last time I'm going to tell you!"

Oh, sure, infancy has its strong points. For instance, when I put Sophie down, I'm reasonably sure she's going to be there when I come back. The same is not true of our son.

"Get down from that cupboard. How'd you get up there? It doesn't matter. Just get down. And close that drawer. You don't *need* a screwdriver. Please put it back. And STOP RUNNING."

So anyway, I just don't know what the big deal is with the terrible twos. They're not so bad. It's this infant stage...

"Oooh, is Mommy's girl sleepy again? There, there, sweetie. You just take another little rest."

—⁓—

WE WERE WATCHING A BASKETBALL GAME the other night when my husband yelled, "Look at that!" I looked up from whatever riveting activity I was doing, perhaps counting the dust bunnies under the sofa, expecting to see some amazing half-court shot or devastating cheerleading accident.

What I saw was a group of mutantly tall young men hovering over a handsome, well-dressed smaller person who must have been the coach, because he didn't seem afraid of them. This coach, I gathered, was the focus of my husband's attention.

"Just look at him!" he cried in disgust, with as much passion as I've heard in his voice in a long time. "He's wearing cuff links with a sports watch! Can you even believe that?!" As if the average person would have noticed.

I looked back at this man to whom I committed my life and distractedly appraised his outfit of choice for the evening, which included a striped dress shirt, plaid pullover sweater, sweat pants with a hole in the thigh, one dress sock, and slippers.

"No, I sure can't," I said, dryly. "How can some people leave the house?"

He looked down at himself, back at me, and growled. He clearly was not amused, and I guess I don't blame him. I know where his buttons are, and I push them. It's what I do.

But then I had to stop and think. Clothes are important to my husband. He's very sensitive about them, as demonstrated by our annual contribution to his dry cleaner's mortgage.

Unfortunately, however, since our new arrival, "well-dressed" in our house means "vomit-free." So he lashed out in disgust over what is to most a detail but to him a fashion faux pas because he himself was sporting a burpy cloth.

What's going on here? I can't help but wonder if maybe we sometimes criticize others for things we struggle with ourselves.

My husband couldn't fault the coach's clothes because he was, in fact, a natty dresser. He dressed the way my husband used to dress, and still does if he can make it out of the house before a child jumps on his back. But it hurt my husband a little to see it, I think, and so he grasped at the only available blemish — the cuff links with the sports watch — as the target of his disdain.

So maybe that's it. Maybe when we see something we want but can't have, it's easier to find fault than to face the fact that we can't have it, for whatever reason that may be. I thought back to when I was a kid and mocked all the little girls with their little monogrammed purses and sweaters. The truth was that I wanted my own little monogrammed stuff but, since I couldn't have it, it was easier to pretend I didn't like it. Worked with boys, too, come to think of it.

So anyway, there I was, all smug and uppity for having successfully analyzed my husband yet again, when it was my turn. He was picking me up from the exercise class to which I've condemned myself, when I pointed out a classmate who was in fantastic shape, beautiful, and nice — in short, everything I currently am not but am struggling to be.

"Look at that woman!" I cried in disgust. "Can you even

believe her?!" I was clearly piqued. My husband glanced her way for what seemed an inordinately long period of time.

"I'm looking, and still trying to find a flaw," he finally said, which anyone knows was not the correct response.

Can't find a flaw, my butt, I muttered to myself. "Just look at her!" I cried. "Don't you see she's got a hair out of place? I mean, really! How can some people leave the house?"

—⁓—

"WELL, YOU LEARN SOMETHING NEW every day." That was my response on the rare occasion when someone corrected me. It took the sting out of the realization that I did not, in fact, know everything, which I believed I did based on the amount of time I've been here.

It's like an honorary degree — you don't actually have to attend the classes to learn the stuff; if you're around long enough, it's just assumed you picked it up along the way. But boy, there's nothing like kids in your life to remind you how very dumb you really are.

I mean, sure, my daughter can't quite speak yet, and my son thinks kissing a booboo makes it better. She thinks soup is more fun to wear than to eat, and he thinks anything before this moment was "yesterday" and anything after is "tomorrow," but when it comes to educating Mommy, they're the best darn teachers in the world. I expect a tuition bill any day now.

And since I've already embarked on this crash course in reality, I thought it might be helpful to share some observations that really are not among those best learned the hard way. Please take notes; there may be a quiz.

∽ Baby-proof your home all you want, but realize that even the softest cushion will hurt if you fall into it with a hairbrush in your mouth.

∽ Don't introduce the concept of monsters to a toddler until you're good and ready to sleep on half of a twin bed for several months.

∽ "Watch the baby" doesn't actually mean watch the baby, as in "watch the baby take a header down the stairs." It means "watch what she's doing and intercept her before she gets hurt."

∽ If you tell a toddler he can watch a movie, give specific choices. Understand that his irrational concept of time does not apply here, and his film choice will invariably be the longest movie ever made.

∽ As long as there is a shelf over your bed to keep the remote, glasses and various books, the concept of napping with a mobile child is a fantasy.

∽ Babies are like crocodiles. They may appear slow and cumbersome, but the minute your head is turned, their teeth are clamped onto your leg.

∽ The preview channel is just as amusing to most children as "Blue's Clues"...although knowing some adults as I do, it could be argued that in this particular case, age isn't the determining factor.

∽ Mirrors are an endless source of intrigue for a young child. And while I'm not saying it's a gender thing, every time my son and I pass a mirror on the wall and I cry "Handsome guy alert!" my husband looks, too.

∽ Shaking the head back and forth means "no." So does nodding it up and down. I've yet to figure out what it means when it spins completely around, but I'm guessing it's not good.

∾ Contrary to Mommy's rather expensive belief, babies don't care what they wear. If they don't voice an opinion on their wardrobe, it's not because they can't talk; it's because they don't have one. Save yourself some cash.

∾ Children have no fear. Everything is fair game. I know the books say this is healthy and such unabashed curiosity should be encouraged but, absent a relatively advanced capacity for upright mobility, I have my doubts. Remember, these same books also said labor was "uncomfortable."

Since the birth of my children, I've been in constant awe of how much they have to learn, wondering if I would be an adequate teacher. And I've been focused so intently on introducing them to life that I almost didn't notice all of the things they're teaching me because, the truth is, when it comes to them, I really know nothing.

Here come the tikes now, so I have to go. Class is in session.

—∾—

MY HUSBAND AND I WERE HAVING the same old argument.

"A list is just that — a list," he said, obviously frustrated. "It is not an outline. It is not a guide just to get you to certain aisles wherein you proceed to drop things willy-nilly into the cart. When you need something, you write it down — hence the list — and when you go the store, you buy it. That's how it works."

This man, whom I adore for his enthusiasm for grocery

shopping, is the only person I know who can go to the store and come home with everything on the list and absolutely nothing else. Nothing. No diversions. No side trips. No extras. It's sick, I tell you.

I, on the other hand, learned the hard way about shopping lists. I would write down everything I used up and make a note of things we were low on until I had a perfect list broken down into store sections. Then, when the time came, I would unfailingly forget. Not the list, mind you. I would forget to go shopping.

And so I learned how to wing it at the grocery store. But one thing never changed. There is one caveat to shopping that is universal. That thing, of course, is cookies.

"All right," I replied. "Let's go over it one more time. Whenever you go to the store, you get whatever you went in for, and cookies. If you go for diapers, you get diapers and cookies. If you go for a billion things, you get those billion things *and cookies*. Cookies never have to be written down. They're a given. That's just how it's always been."

"How did you manage to stay so thin all those years?" he asked me incredulously.

"Well," I said, smugly, "it's a gift, really." Suddenly, however, I caught on to his use of the past tense, and I wasn't so smug anymore.

"And my philosophy on cookies has nothing to do with how long it takes me to lose pregnancy weight. They are completely unrelated issues." I walked away, determined to lose 20 pounds by sunset.

As I stopped by the cookie jar on my way to the ab cruncher, I was again struck by his complete inability to understand something that is so personal to me. And I refuse to believe I'm the only one who holds it as truth. It is The Cookie Theory, and it states as follows:

- If you eat cookies standing up, there are no calories.
- If you eat holiday cookies after the holidays, there are no calories.
- If you break a cookie in two and eat half now and half later, there are no calories.
- If you eat your child's leftover cookies, there are no calories.
- Cookies eaten in the middle of the night have no calories.
- Cookies eaten in the car have no calories.
- Cookies eaten off the floor, with strict adherence to the five-second rule, obviously, have no calories.
- Cookies taken out of the dog's mouth have no calories.
- And of course, there is the Cake Corollary:
- Cake eaten right off of the platter has no calories.

It really is so simple. I think maybe he just doesn't *want* to grasp it. At any rate, the next time he wanted to go shopping I felt compelled to intervene.

"I know!" I said enthusiastically. "Let's all go! It'll be fun! I'll show you what it's like to go grocery shopping, Maggie-style!"

He thought about it for a moment and finally replied, "No, that's OK. You go. I'll stay home and watch the kids. I'm not really feeling up to going anymore."

"What's the matter, honey?" I asked. "Don't you feel well? Are you sick? Do you have a fever or anything?"

"No," he said, "I'm OK. I just don't want to go to the store. Suddenly I'm feeling sort of...listless."

—⚬—

"WHAT COLOR DIS?" OUR DAUGHTER ASKED, holding up a crayon.

"That's blue," my husband answered.

"Oh. What color is dis one?"

"That one's yellow," came the answer.

"How 'bout dis one?"

"Blue."

"No, brown, Daddy," said our daughter.

"Well, honey, actually, it's blue," said Daddy.

Silence. Then, "You go over there." Apparently the child did not care for that last response. She wanted that darn crayon to be brown. And the more I think about it, the more I think she may be on to something. No fuss, no muss. Just "OK, get out." She does the same thing at bedtime.

"Good night, angel," I say.

"Good night, Mommy," she replies.

"I love you," I tell her.

"I love you too, Mommy," she replies.

"Sweet dreams!" I say.

"You too, Mommy," she replies. "Go downstairs."

It's so simple and yet so deep, isn't it? She says what's on her mind. If we say something she doesn't want to hear, she dismisses us. If we say something wrong, she corrects us. If we say something stupid, she laughs at us. It's communication at its most primitive level.

And I think we could learn something from the princess. Her innocent take on life lends a certain clarity to the art of conversation that seems to escape most of us big folk. Age sometimes seems to rob us of the ability to say what we really want to say. Coming from us, it would sound hurtful, mean, or just plain irritating. From our daughter, it's refreshingly honest.

Oh, sure, the theory has its drawbacks. There are times when such refreshing honesty is somehow less than refreshing, times when we really, deep down, wish that kids did not in fact say the darnedest things. In those particular instances, I've learned not to take my cue from a toddler.

For instance, I don't announce when I'm going potty. Nor do I look at someone's thighs and squeal, "Dimples!" And I certainly don't use my little toy shaver on Mommy's whiskers, no matter how long they've gotten in the last year — I mean, jeez, what's *up* with that, anyway? First my butt droops down to my calves, and now I can braid my face. Welcome to 40.

So these are all areas on which my daughter and I disagree when it comes to complete honesty. There are some things I — er, *people* — just don't want to hear.

But otherwise, let it out, that's what I always say. Say what's on your mind. There may even be an amendment or something to that effect. And it's certainly a mainstay in our home, this freedom to speak out. My husband and I practice it regularly, evidenced by my recent undertaking to buy a new car.

"You want that color?" my husband asked. "Are you kidding me? And don't get a stick; they're too much work. What about this one? Sure it's ugly, but what you want is more room, don't you? And I wouldn't go to that place to get it; why not go where I got mine? But, hey, do what you want. It's your car."

I gritted my teeth and replied, "Thank you, honey. That was helpful."

"Oh, and one more thing," he continued. "Get the price down. There's always room to move on these things. Don't settle for the sticker price. And you should get a V-6; it's got more power. And why not get a sunroof this time? But hey, I'm not driving it. Do what you want."

While I appreciated his honest input, I couldn't help borrowing from my daughter's philosophy when I told him where to go.

And of course I meant, "over there."

—⁂—

"SOMEONE'S INTERESTED IN OUR HOUSE," my husband said. "I told them we'd show it this weekend." He then looked at me expectantly.

"That's great!" I replied enthusiastically, thinking he was seeking my approval. He wasn't.

"Do you think we could have it clean by then?" he asked after a long silence.

"You know, honey, that hurts. It really does. It's tough with the kids. I think I do a darn good job keeping this place presentable." I followed his eyes to the dust on the television screen, in which our son had drawn a really quite impressive race track.

"I mean, for the most part," I said lamely. Then I remembered something I had just read about cleaning and allergies.

"Besides, scientists discovered that a certain amount of dirt and dust may actually be helpful in building kids' immune systems! I'm doing our children a great service by not cleaning! You should be thanking me! Look at what we're saving in doctor bills!"

He was muttering as he walked away, but all I could make out was something about "allergic to clean plates."

He's right, of course. I'm not a great housekeeper. I'd love to chalk it up to a fluke of nature and say that I never was, but that's not altogether true. In fact, in the old days, I was borderline anal about neatness. Really. You'd never know it today but, then again, I also used to be a size 2.

Anyway, all you'd have to do is ask my parents. They were there. When I was a child, I cleaned like a madwoman. It's what I did. My brothers played sports, and I vacuumed. And dusted. And washed dishes. And picked up toys. And dusted and vacuumed some more. It was almost scary, I tell you.

But I was my mom's sanity in the maelstrom that was our family. I cleaned whenever I could, as hard as I could. It made my parents happy, and in my mind I won their approval. Turns out they were just thrilled to see the floor, but what did I know? There was some heavy competition for attention in those days. We did what we had to do.

Then, when I got out on my own, I apparently had a revelation of some sort. It occurred to me that all of those years growing up, I felt my worth was somehow attached to my cleaning skills. That's what I associated approval with. My parents loved me because I understood the concept of "elbow grease" and was not afraid to use it.

Oh, sure, my parents felt bad for the misunderstanding, claiming to this day that they loved me for me and not for my cleaning supplies, but the damage was done. I swore off the stuff forever.

I took charge of my self-esteem. When I brought a guy back to my apartment, I would almost dare him to look around. Take me as I am, I would silently declare with a sweep, so to speak, of my arm across a living room adorned in dog hair. I do not clean. I do not cook. I do not do windows. Love me or leave me.

I was single for a long time.

Anyhoo, that may or may not be the origin of my current housekeeping challenge. Who cares, really? My house may be a mess but, darn it, I know my husband loves me for me. And he knows, now, that there are more important things in life than race tracks drawn in the dust. Thank goodness science was there to back me up.

It turns out that the people looking at our house last weekend read the same article. As they went from floor to floor, appraising everything from woodwork to windows, they were very gracious in their comments. When the tour was over, they gave one final look around.

"My!" they said. "What healthy children you must have!"

—⁂—

I WAS WALKING THE DOG THE OTHER night and saw a neighbor coming up her driveway carrying some bags.

"Hey!" I called out cheerily. "What are *you* doing taking out the trash?"

She laughed and replied, "It's not trash. It's my groceries."

"Doh!" I cursed under my breath as I walked away. "What an idiot! Of course it's groceries! Who puts their trash in little tiny plastic bags? And good God — so what if she *was* taking out the trash!" I was mortified. I could see the conversation with her husband — "I just ran into that Maggie down the street... nice enough, but not as progressive as we first thought..."

Darn that poor eyesight! I lamented. In retrospect, I'm pleased I was at least able to distinguish her from her husband. How embarrassing *that* would have been — calling out to the wrong person about something she's not doing and which wouldn't be bad even if she were doing it. A moron in triplicate.

But the truth was even more disappointing. And the truth is, if I'd thought she was her husband, I wouldn't have said what I said, because if I thought she was a he, then in my head the picture wouldn't have seemed odd.

I think what happened was that I had a flashback to my childhood paradigm, in which the boys do the outside work and the girls do the inside work. Back then, my brothers took out the garbage and I did the dishes. That's how it was.

The irony here is that I was afraid to have a daughter, because I rebelled so strongly against that stereotype all of my life that I don't even know how to deal with girls. I don't know how girls are supposed to be anymore. I don't know how to be a mother to one.

And it doesn't matter who told me that boy things were better. What matters is that I believed it. How could I not?

Girls were always trying to be like boys, but I never noticed any of the boys trying to be like girls. In fact, being like a girl was considered mockable — ask anyone who was ever called a "sissy."

I therefore always wore blue jeans, I never wore pink, and I played with trucks. When I got older, I didn't learn to cook, because that was a "girl" thing. And I never cleaned, for the same reason. I got a dog and played football and changed my windshield wipers by myself.

I wanted so much to have what boys have that girl things now have a negative connotation. I'm stuck somewhere on the road to equality, in a place where girls do boy things, and boys do boy things...and no one does girl things, because they're somehow shameful.

But what if my daughter likes Barbies and tea sets and ribbons in her hair? Just because I didn't go for that stuff, does that mean she can't? I watch her twirl around in her beloved tap shoes and pouffy dresses and think, good God, whose child is this...and isn't she just beautiful?

I have to accept the possibility that there's nothing wrong with girl things, as long as we choose them. Back in the old days we didn't have that choice, and occasionally those days come back to remind me that now we do. I have to make sure my daughter knows that. I have to make sure that I know it.

Of course, she's just a toddler. We have some time to work on this — or rather, I do. She doesn't have to do anything except grow up and be happy, and I need to let her do that. I need to let her choose what will make her happy.

And if, someday, she chooses to take out the trash wearing a pink dress, then I need to let her do that too.

—◊—

AH, YES. DAY ONE. I remember it well.

Preschool was still a month away, and vacation was over. My window of opportunity had opened for the ultimate toddler challenge — potty training. My daughter's preschool had sent home specific instructions on the subject, summed up thusly: "Children must be toilet-trained. Absolutely no pull-ups."

I was not fazed. Her brother had trained himself in the space of a weekend. I didn't even have to help, if I recall. He was just ready, as I'm sure she will be. Besides, did you ever see a child in kindergarten wearing diapers? Of course not. They get trained, one way or another.

And I was prepared. She had her Elmo potty seat and her own little soap and towel and stepstool. Her new underpants, sporting every character from Tinkerbell to Dora, were placed strategically low where she could reach them herself. I encouraged her, told her what a big girl she was and how much she was going to enjoy preschool. It couldn't fail.

Day Seven. After a week, I was beginning to think that success might not be as easily attained as I'd first thought. She's a stubborn one, all right. It's a trait that I'm sure will serve her well in years to come, but it's not doing me any favors right now. So I did some reading, and had a few new tricks up my sleeve.

We started with the Ballet Barbie, for which she had pined at a playmate's house. I surprised her with it and said, "Honey, if you go on the potty for two whole days, Ballet Barbie will be yours!" She dutifully went on the potty for two whole days, took her Barbie, and gave it to the dog as a chew toy. She then smiled at me and peed on my rug.

We have since moved to gumballs as the bribe of choice; though not quite as good for the teeth, they are infinitely less expensive. Unfortunately, these are only moderately successful, and one can't help but inhale that telltale odor upon entering our home.

"Gosh, Mag," my husband said. "That smell is really noticeable. Is there any way you could maybe speed up this process, before we have to re-carpet the house?"

I glared at him as only a woman can who has spent way too many hours playing patty-cake with a potty-bound toddler, and said, "I'll have the carpets cleaned. And unless you have some more, shall we say, helpful suggestions, it might behoove you to leave me alone for the next month."

"Can't we confine her to the kitchen or something?" he asked.

"You mean, like a dog?" I asked incredulously.

"Well, I know it sounds bad, but —" he started. He was cut off with a quick dish towel to the head, and left.

Day 21, and we're no closer to long-term success than we were a month ago. I've tried everything, from the bribes to cajoling to pleading to threats. "Honey," I said, "if you don't go on the potty, you can't go to preschool. Don't you want to go to preschool, sweetie?"

She looked at me soulfully, this little thing who has done nothing but sing the praises of preschool for the last four months, and said simply, "No."

"Well, baby, MOMMY NEEDS YOU TO GO TO

PRESCHOOL! OK? Please? Now hop on up. There's my girl."
Yes, one could say that Mommy was getting a little frustrated.

Day 28. So here we are, entering week five. Fortunately my daughter's preschool has a graduated entry system; they go for a half hour the first week, one hour the second, etc. That buys me a little more time. I mean, how long can this last, really?

Day 730. Kindergarten is starting, and this time I mean it. It's going to work. She's going to start using that potty.

—⁓—

MY BODY HAS A MIND OF ITS OWN. Apparently it thinks that "new year" is synonymous with "exercise program," and has been attempting to coerce me into one. Right. Like shifting from one side of the couch to the other isn't work.

"Hey! What about ME?" it asked. "Hello! Down here! The attachment to your neck that is beginning to resemble a marshmallow? Remember? When are we going to join a gym? A girl your age has a lot more than just a reputation to uphold, you know — your butt springs to mind! So when's it going to be? Huh? Huh?"

"Hmmm," I answered thoughtfully. "How about never? Is never good for you?"

"Yeah, ya big coward. That's the thanks I get for silently squeezing into those jeans all these months? I knew you were a weenie."

"I have a black belt, I'll have you know!" I retorted. "You might want to show a little respect! There was a day when the only ripples on my body were the ones defining my abdomen!"

"'Ooh, look at me, I'm a martial artist!' Well, Jean-Claude Van Flab, let's invite reality in for some tea, shall we? That day was FOUR YEARS AGO. Those laurels you're resting on are becoming a little more than figurative. People are gonna start calling you 'Baggie'!"

"My, but you've gotten cocky in your old age," I responded, "considering I'M STILL THE BOSS. I own you. You're mine."

"Gee, boss, I hate to shatter your delusions of adequacy," it shot back, "but your employee is revolting — and you can take THAT any way you want."

I looked down and sighed. It had a point.

"OK, I will concede that there was a time in my life when my arms didn't jiggle when I blow-dried my hair — if YOU will admit there are ways to exercise which don't involve spandex shorts and equipment that can kill you if you look at it wrong."

"Aw, come on!" it taunted. "Bowflex! Nautilus! Buns of Steel! Say it with me!"

"OK, you know what? You need to lay off the infomercials. I have a big dog and two kids under 5 and you don't think I exercise? I chase after a Pink Power Ranger half the day and Jimmy Neutron the other half, and I don't get any exercise? Up and down a four-story house eight times an hour and that's not exercise? You want to talk Stairmaster? I AM the stairmaster!"

"Uh-huh," it said, somewhat sarcastically. "And I'm Cindy Crawford."

"Now that's not fair!" I cried. "So what if she was back to her pre-baby weight in six weeks! She had trainers, and diet specialists, and babysitters, and hair people —"

"Hair people? What's that got to do with her body?"

"Well, nothing," I pouted, "but she had 'em, and it's just not fair!"

"So, you're leaning towards…what, then? The 'nine months on, nine years off' program? Is that it?" This was really beginning to bug me. My own body, biting the hand that feeds it. So to speak.

"OK. All right. You win. You want some action? I'll give you some action." I leaned back to do a side kick. Along the way, bones were crunching, joints were grinding, and muscles were straining in a chorus of what could only be described as poetic torture.

"No! Wait! I was kidding!" it cried. "Ouch! Haven't you ever heard of stretching? I'm sorry! I'll leave you alone! Please, just stop!"

It was too much. I took pity on my poor body, which was obviously experiencing some sort of breakdown. I abruptly cut short my effort to get back in shape in the best interest of all concerned. I exercised, if you will, some compassion.

I mean, that had to burn a calorie, right?

—⁓—

Mom's the Word

A S I LOOK AT MY SON, I never thought myself capable of loving someone so intensely that the mere thought of losing him brings tears streaming down my face. As I gaze at my daughter, I never imagined that someone could make me feel so absolutely complete.

And I never believed that these same children, who literally mean more to me than life itself, could MAKE ME SO NUTS.

There. I said it. Sometimes my children make me crazy. The unbridled energy, the unparalleled curiosity, the unnatural aversion to food and sleep — heck, my children and I couldn't be more different. And yes, I admit that it was all very cute and charming when they were babies. There is little that babies can do that is not cute and charming (with the possible exception, of course, of projectile vomiting. But, hey, that's me.)

But as they age I can't help but notice, for instance, that they don't listen as well. And when they do listen, it's with a little more skepticism than I would like, as though they're debating whether to take me seriously. When they were babies Mommy's word was gold, as far as they were concerned. Lately it's pewter, at best.

While we're on the subject, can someone please explain to me the appeal of the game of chase? Or why it is so blasted simple to make Mommy feel like a dunce? When my son was looking for something recently, I asked where it was the last time he had it. He looked at me as if I were a complete moron and replied, "In my hand." Duh.

Then there was The Rain Conversation with the daughter:

"Mommy, what's rain made of?"

"Water, honey. Water that comes out of the clouds."

"Oh. What's water made of?"

"Uh...hydrogen and oxygen, honey. Mixed together."

"Oh. What's oxygen made of?"

"I don't know, honey. When you learn to read you can look it up."

"OK...Mommy, what're clouds made of?" "AAAAAAAA AGGGGGGGGGGHHHHHHHHHHHHHHHH!!!!!!!!"

And of course the grocery store's always a treat. We were shopping the other day when suddenly my daughter started screaming. My son immediately turned to me, the picture of self-righteous indignation, and cried, "I didn't antagonize her!"

Everyone within earshot laughed at this proclamation. What they missed was my daughter's precious blanket peeking out from under her brother's shirt. So not only did he in fact antagonize her, he knew enough to hide the evidence and profess his innocence. Should I be worried about that, do you think?

Then there was the time when they were younger and I

needed a new outfit for an upcoming event. Generally not one to try things on, I decided that for the price I was going to pay for this dress, it'd better look good. I looked at the kids and thought, well, I'll simply have to risk it.

I went to the first available store, grabbed the first available dress, and headed to the dressing room. So far, so good. We got in and locked the door, and I breathed a sigh of relief. The kids were fascinated by themselves in the mirror, which I realize is an issue all by itself.

I started undressing. Off came the slacks without a hitch (unless you count the somewhat embarrassing need for a shoe-horn to get them over my hips.) I then grasped the bottom of my shirt and yanked it over my head.

And they were gone. They weren't really amused by the mirror; they were merely biding their time until Mommy was temporarily blinded so they could scoot out under the dressing room door like little bugs. And what could I do? Take a moment to get dressed, while my kids wandered alone in a department store?

Of course not. I ran out of the dressing room half naked. I was calling to them while running while putting on slacks while careening off clothes racks. Finally a clerk realized what happened, and when she stopped laughing she grabbed the kids and led them by the hand back to Mommy, who now had one leg in a pair of pants and a shirt draped over her like a Miss America banner.

Oh, well. What can we do? They're kids. They're exploring their world and learning as much as they can and testing their boundaries. It's what kids do. I just have to ride it out. After all, this phase won't last forever, and next thing I know they'll be teen-agers.

And really, how hard can *that* be? Right?

—∞—

IT WAS EARLY MORNING, and I was drinking my coffee on my favorite chair with my dog Decker at my feet. The kids were still sleeping, the husband was outside washing the car, and I had a few precious moments of peace. And then we heard it.

"CHIRP."

It wasn't a cute little chirp like the sound of a robin, however; it was more of a screeching chirp like that of a huge parrot on whose foot a 30-pound rock has just landed. My startled dog stood up and looked around for the unseen enemy but found none. He then lay back down, apparently deciding the best defense was a good nap. Again, the shrill call.

"CHIRP."

It sounded like it was coming from a wall hanging, which made no sense at all since it wasn't even a picture of a bird. Then I noticed a smoke detector on the ceiling nearby. When my husband came in, I made a joke of it and said, "Honey, either we have a really large bird stuck in our wall, or the smoke detector needs a new battery!"

He glanced up at what I presumed to be the offending item and said, "These don't use batteries. They're electric." He then retreated back to the relative sanity of the car, leaving the dog and me to our nightmarish imaginations as to what might actually be in the wall.

Later that same day my 4-year-old raced up from the

playroom and announced, "Tom and Jerry are barking." Tom and Jerry, of course, are frogs.

"Honey," I replied patiently, "frogs don't bark. The standard frog sound is a ribbit."

She looked at me as though I were a moron, and finally said, "I know that, Mom. That's why it was so funny that they barked."

Let me just add here that frogs were not my idea for pets. My husband took the kids out one day to look at fish in the pet store, and came home with two frogs and a little frog house that apparently can only be cleaned and maintained by a specially trained person, in this house referred to as a "mom."

And while I typically prefer pets that can either catch a frisbee or use the toilet, I nevertheless helped the kids to set up proper quarters for the little guys — dubbed Tom and Jerry by The Boy Who Claims He Does Not Watch Too Much Television — down in the playroom.

We filled their tank with the requisite dirt and sticks, and gave them a bowl of water. "Oh, I forgot," I said to my husband when we were done decorating. "What do they eat?"

Edging suspiciously toward the stairs, he quickly said, "Live crickets," and sprinted up three at a time.

Gee, I don't know why he thought that would upset me. I mean, it's not as though I would be the one buying those live crickets every week, right?

So anyway, as long as I was stymied by the upstairs chirping, I thought I should probably investigate the little downstairs phenomenon. I found my 6-year-old in the playroom, studiously examining the tank. "I don't see a dog in there," he finally said. "And actually, I only see one frog; I think it's Tom. Or Jerry. Whichever he is, the other one must still be hiding."

I didn't have the heart to remind him that one of the frogs has been "hiding" for several months, and after noting the paunch on the remaining Tom-or-Jerry, made a mental note to find out what the frogs eat if, for instance, someone once forgot to get their crickets.

Suddenly I heard a distinctive bark. I quickly glanced at the dog, who looked up defiantly with his teeth clenched. "OK, OK," I said. "I was just checking. Jeesh." I then started looking around the tank for an errant barking toy, finding none. I did notice, however, that the tank lid was slightly open.

"That's it!" I cried triumphantly. "The chirping upstairs must be a cricket that got out! He must have gotten behind that picture and can't get out." I was really quite proud of my deductive reasoning, until my son said, "Uh, Mom, what about the barking frog?"

"Well," I said, "that's a mystery for another day. Don't want to overdo, do we?" I turned toward the stairs and said, "Come on, Deck. Let's go celebrate with a treat." To which I could swear he replied...

"Ribbit!"

—⚉—

MY MOTHER LIFEGUARDS at the community pool in my hometown, and each year she wrestles with the fact that the other lifeguards, most of them 50 years her junior, don't enforce safety rules. She feels like an outcast because she routinely does enforce them. She is, after all, guarding lives. And she's a mother. The two are often linked.

"One of the rules," she once said, "is this: 'No Frisbees, no balls, no inflatable toys allowed in the pool area.' So today these kids were throwing around a thing called a 'squishy,' a water ball. I asked the young guard of that section if she was going to step in, and she said no, that it wasn't a ball, it was a squishy."

My mother was beside herself.

"Of course it's a ball!" she cried. "It's a Squishy ball! It's a flying projectile that could hit an unsuspecting swimmer in the face! The fact that Squishies are not specifically listed in the rules as banned does not mean they're allowed! The assumption is that no balls means no flying objects!"

I felt bad for her, but what I'm finding with kids is this: There are no valid assumptions. There are no generalities. There are no broad categories or all-encompassing groups to which dangerous things can be assigned and then banned so that our children will be safe. Children think in specifics.

For example, and I'm not saying this has happened in my house, but imagine telling your child, "Please don't throw blocks at your sister's head."

Sounds pretty straight-forward, doesn't it? Of course it does. You're an adult. But what a child hears is this:

"Don't throw blocks at your sister's head. You may, however, throw them at her face, back, stomach, arms, legs and feet." Or this:

"Don't throw blocks at your sister's head. You may, however, throw trains, dolls, remotes, bowls, sippy cups or anything else within reach at her head."

Do you see how one simple rule can be interpreted in many different ways by the inexperienced — and determined — ear?

The phrase, "It goes without saying" should never enter the realm of children, because in their lives, nothing goes without saying. You can't just say, "Please pick up your clothes," because the clothes could end up on the dog's head. If you want them to put the clothes in the laundry basket, you must say, "Please pick up your clothes and put them in the laundry basket."

And interestingly, I find that the phenomenon can actually get worse before it gets better. My son is not quite old enough to understand the concept of "including but not limited to," but is right on top of the "well, she didn't say I couldn't do THIS" rationalization.

"Mommy!" my daughter cries from the backyard after I send them out to play. "He's using me as home plate!"

"Please don't use your sister as home plate," I call to my son.

"OK," he calls back.

"Mommy!" cries the girl. "He's using me as first base!"

"Well, you didn't tell me I couldn't," he calls after.

(Sigh.) "OK. Don't use your sister as first base, second base, third base, or home. Don't use her as a bat, and don't use her as a backstop. That about cover it?" I call to the boy.

I don't mind saying I get a little weary trying to account for every possible scenario, every possible eventuality or outcome for every instruction I give my children. I find it particularly tiresome on those days when I can barely remember my own name, let alone try to predict how the command of "Please wipe your feet" could be interpreted.

In the long run, I'd prefer my kids be creative and clever

rather than follow each and every command without question. But I'm also learning that they need to hear the words: "Be fair. Be kind. Don't smoke. Don't do drugs. Don't be a bully. Be a good friend. Help others. Try your best." I'm learning that whether you're a parent or a lifeguard — and if you're a parent, then you ARE a lifeguard — then there is at least one valid assumption.

If something goes without saying...then it probably needs to be said.

—∞—

"SO, IS HE READY TO GET on the bus?" my friend asked, knowing my son is starting kindergarten. "And, more important, are *you*?"

"He sure is, but last I checked, *I'm* not getting on the bus!" I laughed, fully aware of her meaning but not quite prepared to answer. What she meant, of course, was, am I ready for my son to get on the bus? And, of course, I'm not.

I don't know what it is about the simple act of climbing those steps, but the mere thought of it induces an almost physical ache in my heart. Maybe it's because the first bus ride is somehow symbolic of growing up and, despite the giddy anticipation with which I have envisioned my children heading off to kindergarten, the truth is that, like many parents, I'm simply not ready to let him go.

Or, more likely, I'm not ready to stop protecting him. Once he steps on that bus, I can no longer pretend for him that there is no bad in the world.

This little guy has been sheltered from birth. I've essentially censored what he watched and what he heard, so that nothing scary or profane pierced that fragile shell of innocence. I've been committed to providing my son with a childhood in which love, safety, security and respect were unconditional and unqualified; a childhood in which happiness is the norm and hurt the exception.

All of these thoughts were swirling around my head recently when I took my son to our local daily recreation program. We were late getting there. He signed in, took his little lunchbox to the area reserved for the younger kids, gave me a quick peck on the cheek, and was gone, off to the playground in search of a friend. For some reason I held back, watching.

He climbed the rope ladder, went down the slide, and stood there, looking around. His closest friend, I remembered, had left for vacation and wouldn't be there, but he didn't know this. And because we were late, little groups had already formed in the different areas of the playground.

Unaware of my presence, he looked from group to group for a familiar face, while my heart started splintering with each passing second at the thought of him being excluded.

My son is a nice little boy. He is empathic, and considerate, and very sensitive, and in my experience, this translates into a person who is hurt easily. I realize that a certain amount of pain builds character and is a part of life, but as he stood there that morning, surveying the clusters of children that had already formed, I wanted to run over, take his hand, and bring him home. Of course I knew I couldn't.

And as I watched, a little boy stood up from the sandbox, walked over to my son, and handed him a shovel. The boy then went to get himself another tool, and they both sat down in the sandbox and started digging.

Frozen in my spot on the path, I exhaled and realized I hadn't taken a breath throughout the entire scene. The relief that swept over me was so dramatic that I almost wept, and that reaction led me to conclude that something else was going on.

And suddenly I knew what it was.

I wasn't watching him on that playground looking for a friend...I was watching me, or at least the little girl I once was. My heart was breaking because I knew the pain of being excluded, of being on the fringe, of being the last picked in gym. I knew the anxiety of being on the outside, of constantly questioning my self-worth. I knew the fear of climbing those steps to the bus and wondering what nightmare awaited me that day.

Being hurt — being excluded — being an outsider...I thought those were my fears for my son. But as I watched him with his new playmate, I have to admit I didn't see any of the self-doubt or insecurity that was so consuming in myself. Those fears, then, aren't for him. Those are my fears for me, that little girl, because that was my life.

The painful experiences of my childhood, dulled over the years, made me the person — and the mother — I am today. But I have to stop projecting them onto my son, because my experience will never be his. I've worked on myself for a long, long time to ensure that very truth. Now, however, I have to let him have his own.

Since the day he was born my husband and I have been getting ready for this moment. We've made him feel safe, secure, and loved. In all his young life he has had not one reason to doubt our faith in him, not one reason to feel ashamed, not one reason to wonder if he's worthwhile. And it shows. He wasn't panicking that day at the playground; I was. He was just standing there looking for a friend.

I made a joke of it, but there's some truth there after all. I'm not getting on that bus. My son is. And yes...we're ready.

— ∕∕∕ —

THE KIDS WERE PLAYING house the other day, and I listened surreptitiously as I brought up from the basement box after box of Christmas decorations, delighted at their ability — at least at that moment — to get along. The scene was a classic; my son was playing father, my daughter was playing mother, and their stuffed animal friends were playing the 400 siblings that my children apparently want.

As I continued my happy task of preparing for the season, I thought, this is really quite nice. This is how it's supposed to be.

The kids then wrapped up their scenario and were preparing for the next, when my daughter proclaimed, "This time I want to be the daddy."

My son, the older and wiser of the two, said simply, "No."

My daughter then said, slightly louder, "I want to be the daddy!"

"You can't be the daddy," my son said calmly. "You're a girl. Girls are mommies."

At this point my daughter, whose screams can actually shatter glass in the house next door, screamed, "I DON'T WANT TO BE THE MOMMY!"

No longer calm, my son half-shouted, half-cried, "WELL, I DON'T WANT TO BE THE MOMMY EITHER!"

I felt the need to intervene. "Excuse me!" I called. "I'm in the room, you know!"

"If you won't be the mommy, then I won't play with you!" pouted my daughter, my girlfriend, my biggest fan.

"Well, if YOU won't be the mommy, then I won't play with YOU!" replied my son, my little man, my supposedly sensitive one. And they both stomped off to their rooms, leaving me with a pile of dusty ornaments, tangled lights and more than a passing curiosity about what, exactly, was so wrong with being the mommy.

I began to assess what my children's most likely image of me would be. I thought about my life and my role as they may appear to young minds, and made a shocking discovery. Seeing it through their eyes, even I wasn't sure I wanted to be the mommy anymore.

And there are several reasons for which I can understand them opting for the daddy role. First of all, between the two of us, I'm certainly not the better-dressed. I glanced down at my current garb — drawstring sweats with a hole in the knee, permanently coffee-stained T-shirt with a hole, somehow, in the sleeve, and white yet unmatching socks.

I then recalled my husband as he left for work that morning — showered, shaved and downright handsome in his suit and tie.

I then tried to envision, through the kids' eyes, what we do. Mommy's list includes getting each child up in the morning, preparing and cleaning up breakfast, jumping into whatever clothes are handy, with "clean" and "attractive" a far distant consideration; helping each child get dressed and getting them to and from various pre-schools; setting up and cleaning up Play-Doh, painting and coloring projects; preparing and cleaning up lunch; grocery shopping; laundry; vacuuming up the almost unnaturally accumulating dog hair; trying to work while the children are playing "Let's Make a Band" with the pots and pans; dusting; preparing and cleaning up dinner; bathing and getting the children ready for bed; and folding laundry.

My husband's day, to my children, looks something like this: Get up, make coffee, take a shower, put on a nice suit, and leave. Come home at dinnertime, read to kids.

Yes, from that perspective, I can see how they'd rather be the daddy. What I realized is that, at their young age, there are two major gaps in their vision. The first gap is what their daddy does when he leaves the house, which they will someday understand. The second is why Mommy does what she does, which they may or may not someday understand.

What matters, really, is that I finally understand it.

When I was a kid, I got presents for Christmas. I remember being happy just because I loved Christmas. I loved the season, first and foremost; but also, I loved presents.

As I got older, however, an ever-so-subtle change crept into my once-joyous holiday. While the traditions continued, over the years it became more and more apparent that something was missing. There was a "perfect present" out there, an elusive gift that would somehow make Christmas complete again. I didn't know what it was, but I knew I wanted it.

Then one day I had kids. All at once, Christmas was filled

with something completely different, something I'd missed so vaguely and yet so desperately all those years, something completely other than me...it was filled with awe, and excitement, and unconditional happiness. It was filled with these children.

It was there, this spirit, in every Christmas present, every Christmas song, every Christmas story. And one day I realized, after Christmas had passed, that I didn't have the usual letdown, the usual vague sense that I didn't get what I wanted. I realized that I finally received that elusive gift. I finally knew what it was that I'd wanted all those years. And I'm sure my kids would laugh, if only they understood.

Because, unlike them, I wanted to be the mommy.

—⁓—

MY HOMETOWN GIRLFRIEND AND I were having our semi-annual chat recently, and after updating me on family matters, she began to regale me with stories of her three dogs in the snow. After a moment, I had to interrupt.

"Sandy," I said, "did I miss something? Last time we talked, I could've sworn you only had two dogs."

"Oh, yes, well," she replied, somewhat sheepishly. "We actually got another one in the fall. I haven't told very many people, because they'll think we're crazy!"

After hanging up I thought, well, that's just a sad state of affairs, if you can't talk about things you do for fear of other people's judgment. Besides, the only people who would think she's crazy were those who don't love dogs. No dog people in their right minds would even question it.

With that little profundity came yet another, more disturbing realization: It's almost the same situation with parenthood. I have found myself, on that rare occasion, doing things as a parent that I wouldn't necessarily volunteer into conversation at, say, a business dinner. In fact, if I'd known parents who did these same things before I myself became a parent, I would have probably thought them very bad parents.

And I'm not even talking about extreme-circumstance, once-in-a-lifetime behavior. I'm talking about the kinds of things that help get us through the day. I'm talking about letting my kids eat popsicles for breakfast because, hey, it's better than the nothing they usually eat, right?

Of course right. We all do things that may or may not have been specifically referred to under the "recommendations" section of a parenting manual. Oh, sure, we might not be 'fessing up in the veggie section of the grocery store, but that doesn't mean it isn't so. And it certainly doesn't mean that other parents would not approve.

And to prove my point, I decided to test my theory on another such parent, one whom I would have thought was a good parent before I had kids, and whom I now think is absolutely awesome. I needed validation from one whose skills are, in my view, at least above reproach, if not downright Ozzie-and-Harriet.

As I homed in on my victim — er, subject — however, my bravado began to fade. She's intelligent and patient and kind, everything one would expect a perfect mother to be. What if I was wrong? What if I AM the only mother in the history of the world to let her infant cry in his crib for 15 minutes because if she didn't have a shower she was going to lose her ever-lovin' mind? The humiliation would be unbearable.

I therefore decided on a subtle approach, to kind of feel her out for her reaction.

"Hi," I said on the phone. "How are you? What's the weather out your way? How's work? Really? Great! You know, sometimes when my son wets the bed in the middle of the night, I just put a towel over it until morning."

My friend was quiet for a moment, and then offered, "If my 3-year-old is really tired, sometimes I let her go to bed without brushing her teeth..." and added, "Heck, sometimes I don't brush *my* teeth."

Wow, I thought to myself. That's a good one. I wonder if we should delve into the "How many baths a week are enough?" issue...nah. Next time.

"I bribed my son with a new bike if he'd start going to bed without me laying down with him," I said.

Quiet again. "I let my daughter play with a box of Band-Aids, covering both her legs with them, because it kept her entertained for 20 minutes."

"Wow —" I started, only to be cut off.

"But wait, there's more," she said. "I left them on her for days because I didn't want to deal with her screaming while I pulled them off." I could envision the sigh of relief, the weight that is lifted upon confession of long-held misdeeds.

And it went from there. Parent after parent, confession after confession, burden after burden. Perceived transgressions ranged from heating baby's bottle in the microwave to driving around at night to put a child to sleep. And with each one I gave a supportive nod and smile. I believe what happened was a cross between "confession is good for the soul" and "misery loves company."

Whatever the process became, it certainly validated both my mom and me. When I was a teen-ager and my youngest siblings were born, I remember grocery shopping with my mom and watching in awe as she opened a box of vanilla wafers and let the babies eat them while we shopped. I also remember thinking, "Yikes. I will NEVER let my kids do that."

The translation, if you will allow me, was as follows: "I love my mother dearly and acknowledge that while she did a pretty good job with us older kids, she is obviously slipping on the second batch. I'm sure when and if it's my turn to have children, I will be much better at it."

Years later, the inevitable occurred...she came shopping with us. One minute she was admiring my children's cherubic faces, the next she couldn't even find them. White donut powder covered every square inch. Their eyes and mouths were still visible, which was at once a relief and somewhat horrifying. But my mom had her moment. She realized that I finally understood. And she was happy.

After all of that research, it would seem that my theory on "kid people" might have some truth to it — that other parents and caregivers have done and lived through things that would not necessarily be found in the "What to Expect" books. So come on, people — let it out! There's no need to hide! Tell the world that your child is old enough and clever enough to change her own diapers and still isn't potty-trained! Oh, wait — that's me. Never mind.

The point is that my friend with the dogs will hopefully come to realize that other dog people will not think her crazy for having three dogs, and that other parents — and I — will hopefully realize that despite our insecurities and fear of judgment, we all, for the most part, understand popsicles for breakfast.

—⚶—

EXCUSE ME! EXCUSE ME! If you all could please take your seats, the show is about to begin. Thank you!

Tonight you will have the special privilege of viewing the first of what we're guessing — ! — will be an ongoing performance. It stars two up-and-comers with, if you will forgive the favoritism, tremendous talent. I have no idea from where it comes, but it certainly is not hereditary. It should be noted that the evening will end early. The stars go to bed at 8 p.m.

At any rate, sit back, relax, and enjoy the show. It's a little something we like to call, "Histrionics? What Histrionics?!"

Act One — The Boo-Boo

"Mommy, I have a boo-boo!" cries 3-year-old.

"Where?" Mommy asks.

Daughter points to her shin. "Right here. Don't touch it!"

"I just want to see it, honey. Did you fall?"

"No! Don't touch it!"

"Well, how did it happen? Is it a scra—"

"Don't touch it!"

"Sweetie, it just looks like a little piece of grass. Let me brush — "

"NO! DON'T TOUCH IT!"

"Honey, it's not a boo—"

"DON'T TOUCH IT!" Daughter runs from the room screaming. End of Act One.

Act Two — The Pirate

"Mommy, Andy has a pirate costume — *with* pants," reports 5-year-old. "His mom *made* them."

"That's cool! He's so lucky! Did he let you try it on?" Mommy enthusiastically replies.

"Yes, and it was *very* cool. Did I tell you his mom made it?"

"You did mention that, honey. She must be very clever!"

"Can you make a pirate costume?" son inquires.

"Gosh, I don't know, sweetie. Mommy's not that handy with a sewing machine. But you've got your sword and eye patch — "

"But you'll TRY to make a pirate costume, right?"

"Well, honey, I'm not sure my sewing machine even works — "

"Mom. It's not very hard. Just try it."

"I'm sure it's not very hard, but I'm not sure — "

"Mommy, I'm serious. I have to have a pirate costume. Today." Short pause. "Please."

"All right, hon, I'll look around for some things we could use —"

"MOMMY! IF I DON'T HAVE A REAL PIRATE COSTUME TODAY I WILL DIE."

Son runs from room screaming. End of Act Two.

Act 3 — Well, I Didn't Do It!

(Crash heard as lamp is knocked to floor.)

"What was that?" Mommy calls from kitchen.

"What was what?" children respond innocently.

"What was that crash in the family room?" Mommy asks, patiently.

"Sophie did it!" son replies.

"Renny did it!" daughter replies.

"I didn't ask who did it," Mommy says. "I asked what it was."

Silence, as though children deep in thought.

"Lamp," they call, simultaneously.

Mommy heaves audible sigh. "What *happened* to the lamp?" she asks.

Silence. Then, "It fell," the children reply.

"How did it fall?" Mommy asks.

"Sophie did it!" son yells.

"Renny did it!" daughter yells.

"Well, you started it!" son yells, accusingly.

"Did not! You did!" daughter smartly replies.

"Oh, for the love of —"

"OW! HE TOUCHED ME!"

"OW! SHE TOUCHED ME!"

"All right, that's it. You — on the couch! You — on the chair! I've had it! What does a mother have to do to get a straight answer around here?! I JUST WANT TO KNOW WHAT HAPPENED TO THE LAMP! AND STOP KICKING THAT BALL! KEEP IT UP AND YOU'LL BE READY FOR YOUR DRIVER'S LICENSE BEFORE THIS TIME-OUT IS OVER!" Mommy runs from room screaming.

End of Act Three.

Anyway, as I said at the start of the show, they're naturals, aren't they? I sure don't know where that dramatic flair comes from, but wherever they got it, they sure got it! Let's give 'em a big hand! There will be more performances as time goes on, we suspect, as our stars get older, louder and more independent. And of course, the good news is they'll get to stay up later, too! Woohoo!

—∞—

THE SPIDER WAS CRAWLING on the floor in the hall, next to where my daughter was putting on her shoes. The eight-legged demon having recently joined her list of childhood fears, I quickly grabbed a napkin and ran over. I scooped it up and put it outside, and came back to help her tie her shoes. She looked up at me with something close to awe.

"Wow, Mommy," she said. "You're not afraid of spiders?"

In that brief instant, I was her hero. I was a giant. I was The Mommy Who Picked Up a Spider. In her eyes, at that moment, I could do no wrong, because I had no fear. And as I looked into those big, beautiful blue eyes, I thought, oh, sweetie. If you only knew. Mommy's afraid of a lot of things.

And, unfortunately, the things I fear can't be picked up with a napkin and thrown outside. They can't be dealt with in therapy or treated with Prozac. They're not the kind of fears that make me scream out loud — usually, or that I even really consciously think about. They're simply there, on some level, all the time. They're my parenthood fears, which started the day I gave birth.

For example, I'm now afraid of cars. I'm afraid because they're so big and our kids are so small and they go so darn fast on our quiet little street, and I'm afraid that one day a ball might go flying out into that street right when a car's coming too fast around that bend, and that one of our kids will go flying out after it.

I'm afraid of necklaces that can choke and plastic bags that can suffocate. I'm afraid of swimming pools and trampolines and baseball bats; of monkey bars and swing sets and bicycles; of football tackles and soccer kicks and tennis serves. I'm afraid of my adolescent children succumbing to peer pressure and of my teen-age children riding in cars with teenage drivers.

I'm afraid of bullies, of kids who might physically or emotionally hurt my children. I'm afraid of older kids saying mean things to them, or teasing them, or making them cry. I'm afraid of not being there when they need to face things on their own — or worse, caving in and helping them, so that they never learn to face them.

I'm afraid of indulging my kids to the point that they don't appreciate what they have, and of denying them to the point that they feel unworthy. I'm afraid of hurting them with my words when I'm angry, and not loving them enough with those words when I'm not.

I'm afraid of the insecurity, depression, low self-esteem and lack of self-worth that I may unwittingly pass onto my children, afraid of knowing that I can't give what I don't have and that I chose to have kids anyway; afraid of the heartache that's in store for them if I can't fix this broken part of me before it's too late. I'm afraid of hurting them with my own flaws.

I'm afraid of illness, and disease, and death. I'm afraid of the pain and the perpetual ache they will feel when my children lose their grandparents. I'm afraid of my own death, of not being here to watch my children grow up, not being here for them through each stage, each new beginning as they become the incredible adults I know they will be. I'm afraid of the devastation they would face in losing their mommy or daddy.

I'm afraid of turning my back in the store some day, or after an argument later in life, and finding my children gone. I'm afraid of not doing exactly the right things for them, of not saying the right things, of not knowing what the right things are. I'm afraid of being afraid, afraid of my own humanness, and of knowing that because of it, I will never be a perfect role model or a perfect mother.

So you see, Mommy's afraid of many things. But no, my angel. Not spiders.

—␣␣—

I REMEMBER ONCE READING something about kids, a little quip to the effect that we spend the first few years of their lives teaching them to stand up and talk, and the next 15 telling them to sit down and be quiet. And I thought, well, that won't be us. My husband and I want our kids to have their own minds and the ability to speak them. We want them to be curious and clever and creative. We will encourage dialog and discussion wherever we can.

And our plan would've worked, too, if not for the fact that our children actually did learn to speak. I apparently had been laboring under the misconception that while I was doing all of my encouraging, discussing, etc., etc., they'd still be drooling into burpy cloths. But no. Once again reality knocked and said, "Hi! May I come in?!"

It started innocently enough, as such things do. We were

finishing dinner and I thought it would be a good time for a Family Discussion, a Serious Talk wherein I impart to our progeny some tidbit of truth or wisdom of which I find them deserving and they respond with thoughtful queries until both sides' concerns are assuaged.

In full Maternal Guidance Mode, I said, "Hey, kids, I have a new safety rule, OK? If the doorbell rings, don't answer it if Mommy's taking a shower."

My husband drew his chair up close to me, reinforcing our unity on the subject. My kids looked at both of us blankly, then at each other, then at the dog. They had no idea what I was talking about, or why.

"What I mean is, if you're downstairs watching a show or doing homework or eating or whatever, and Mommy's upstairs in the shower or not available, and the doorbell rings, just don't answer it. It's not safe."

A few more seconds of blankness, and then the boy came to. "What do you mean, if you're 'not available'? Like if you're stuck in a closet or something?"

I looked at my husband for support and he gave me his best, 'honey, you can do this' look. Turning back to the boy, I said, "Yes, if I was stuck in a closet, that would certainly make me unavailable. But the point really is that I don't want either of you to answer the door if Mommy or Daddy isn't right there with you."

"But what if it's Jason?" asked the boy, referring to his friend down the street.

"Well, Jason doesn't drop by unexpectedly, and if I knew he was coming, I'd make sure I was available, OK?" It was a perfectly reasonable question, I thought, followed by a similarly reasonable reply. This was going splendidly.

"OK, but what if he just wants to borrow a video game?" continued the boy.

"Well, then, you'd have to ask him to come back in a little while." I was maintaining composure because I am, after all, Super Mommy. But then it was my daughter's turn.

"But what if it's Emme?" she asked. "What if she wants to play?"

"Well, honey, Emme wouldn't just drop by either, for goodness sake; she lives on the other side of town! So it really wouldn't be —"

"But what if I played with Emme at school one day," suggested the girl, "and told her that if she ever wanted to come to my house to play, she could, and so she asked her mom if she could and her mom said yes —"

"But Mom, what if —" interrupted the boy.

"HEY!" shouted the girl. "I'M NOT DONE! So what if I played with Emme at school one day and told her that if she ever wanted to come to my house to play, she could, and so she asked her mom if she could and her mom said yes and so she put on shorts and a no-sleeve shirt and her mom drove her over here, and Emme just got out of the car and her mom didn't and her mom drove away and Emme was standing at the front door all by herself?"

As the children went back and forth with potential scenarios that would invalidate the rule, my husband and I watched, mere line judges in this bizarre verbal tennis match.

The boy seized upon our silence. "Hey, I know!" he cried.

"What if it was Mick or Maggie from next door? They can always come in, right?"

"Well, you could let them in, I suppose..." I was faltering.

"Or how about this," he continued enthusiastically. "What if it's Mick or Maggie and they need something from the top shelf of the pantry and I could get it by dragging the counter stool over and standing up on it, even though you've told me never to drag the counter stool over to the pantry and stand up on it?"

"Ooh, ooh, I know!" said the girl. "What if —"

"THAT'S ENOUGH!" I shouted. "NO MORE! JUST DON'T ANSWER THE DOOR!" I crumpled into my husband's shoulder. It was over, finally. The kids watched me for a moment, took their plates up to the sink, and walked away.

"Hey, kids?" I called weakly after them, "Thanks for the chat! Let's do it again real soon, OK?!"

——

RIGHT NOW, THIS VERY MINUTE, as I'm writing this, a little yellow bird is tapping on my window. He's been doing it for three days now. Tap, tap, tap, fly away. Tap, tap, tap, fly away.

At first I thought he might be attacking his reflection, mistaking it for another bird. Then I realized that couldn't be the case, since the window upon which he's fixated is a second-story foyer window which has not been cleaned since we moved in. It's probably the one window in my house in which this bird has no hope of ever seeing his reflection.

So that made me think that maybe he was trying to tell me to wash my windows, but why would it matter to a little yellow bird whether or not my windows are clean? Is he part of the Clean Window Brigade? A spy from my homeowner's association? Did my *mother* send him?! "Tell her I'll hire somebody!" I cried to him. Tap, tap, tap.

And then I remembered reading Einstein's definition of insanity — doing the same thing over and over and expecting different results. Well, guess what? I'm beginning to think this bird is just plain crazy. Crazy as a loon, I think to myself. Or at least as crazy as a small bird with a yellow chest and black wings and tail feathers...loon sounds better.

"Hey, honey," I call to my husband in the next room. "Look at this crazy bird. He's still here. He's still tapping. Isn't that funny? I mean, what's he doing? He keeps hitting his beak on the glass and the same thing keeps happening — nothing! Ha ha ha. Silly bird."

I chuckle as I make my way back to the family room, where my daughter is engaged in her favorite activity of seeing how long she can antagonize her brother before he books a ticket to another planet. It's actually an impressive display from a 5-year-old, between the jumps, the kicks, the twirls, and the myriad of voices she can imitate. All the poor brother wants to do is relax.

"First I'll just jump over your head like this," she says, channeling SpongeBob, "and then I'll try the 360-degree, double triple in-the-air flying double front kick —"

Time to intervene. "Sophie, don't do it," I say.

"— and from there I'll do a quadruple flip — Let the rain fall down and cover me — let it wash away my sanity —" She's changed to Hilary Duff. Except I bet Hilary Duff doesn't completely ignore her mother.

"Sophie," I say, a little louder, "don't jump like that around your brother's head. One of you will get hurt."

"— and then I'll play the drums on your head! Won't that be neat?" Happy, perky Jimmy Neutron voice. Do my kids watch a little too much television? Oh yes. But that's an issue for another day. Today, my daughter is honing her skill of pretending I don't exist. As a talent, it would be enviable — in someone other than my child.

"THAT'S ENOUGH," I yell. "STOP. DOING. THAT. RIGHT. NOW. DO YOU HEAR ME?"

She glares at me. "Of course I do," she replies coolly. "How can I not hear you when...you're...*YELLING* AT ME?"

She then goes right back to what she was doing. "Tap, tap, tap," my husband whispers as he walks by.

And then I get it. Suddenly I picture myself at my dirty window, wondering why nothing is happening as I repeatedly bang into it.

Different kids respond to different things. Though her ability to reduce me to yelling is truly a gift, my daughter does not respond to it. In retrospect, I have found that she responds better to time-outs in a quiet place, and yet that tactic is not usually in my repertoire because it's actually my own personal dream; a quiet moment in a quiet place is what I wish for, so how could it possibly be a punishment?

At any rate, it's something to think about. I'm not saying I'm crazy or anything, because you won't see me tapping on my foyer window anytime soon. But hey, you know what they say.

If the beak fits...

I WAS WATCHING MY SON in karate class the other day, and when it was done, Sherry, one of the instructors, came over and said, "Your son is such a delight! You must be a wonderful mother!"

I beamed with pride. "Yes, he's a good kid," I said. "Thank you so much. For saying so, I mean. That was really nice." I was still beaming as I walked away. Who wouldn't be, after hearing such lovely praise about a son or daughter?

As my head shrunk back down to size, I remembered the second half of Sherry's compliment. What a wonderful thing to say to a parent, I thought to myself. We all want to believe that we're doing a good job. Of course, it would be even more wonderful if it were true.

Because the truth is, I don't think I'm a wonderful mother.

A decent mother? Sure. An adequate mother? Absolutely. But a wonderful mother? Not so much.

Once I thought about it, I could think of nothing else. What exactly is a wonderful mother, anyway? Is she June Cleaver, wearing the dress while making dinner for Ward and the boys? Or Shirley Partridge, the hip single mom who has never had a visible meltdown? How about Claire Huxtable, with nary a hair out of place after a hard day of lawyering and evening of parenting?

Those are some of the standards I grew up with, and I'm reasonably certain I don't fit them. To remove all doubt, I decided to make a list of those qualities that seem to make wonderful mothers, and determine whether I possess those qualities. What I determined is that I never even had a chance. I had kids, not a lobotomy.

∽ **Wonderful mothers are very patient.** OK, let's take a moment to define "very," shall we? Ha ha ha... Actually, while I may not be very patient at times, I am at least working on becoming aware of when I'm being impatient. Hey, one step at a time, people. One step at a time.

∽ **Wonderful mothers are selfless.** This is a tough one for me. On the one hand, I would give — and have given — the shirt off my back for my kids. I will relearn the math that I successfully avoided for 25 years because I know I'm expected to help with homework. I will sit up all night in the rocking chair in my daughter's room when she doesn't feel well. I will drive my children to karate and soccer and ballet and basketball and play dates and preschool and science fairs, and I will do all of this without even thinking twice.

On the other hand, I simply will not buy live crickets to feed to Tom and Jerry, the frogs my husband bought in apparent guilt over the death of last year's goldfish. Needless to say, he has since been barred from shopping without me...unless he's shopping for live crickets.

∽ **Wonderful mothers iron their children's clothes.** We stopped at my mother-in-law's house one day and she was in the middle of ironing. My son looked at the iron and board with great curiosity and finally asked, "Grandma, what are you doing?" The look she shot me was one I will not soon forget, let me tell you. And for the record, I don't send my kids out in wrinkled clothes. If they get wrinkled, I give them away. They would've outgrown them anyway.

∽ **Wonderful mothers (see June Cleaver, above) cook real meals three times a day, almost every day.** Hey, this one's just not fair, OK? I don't like to cook. Therefore I am bad at it. My husband knew it when he married me and has never once complained (to my face.) My children should've known it when they were born to me.

The good news is, they are both gifted with amazing memories for phone numbers, and can practically order takeout all by themselves, bless their little hearts. I'm so darn proud of 'em.

- **Wonderful mothers don't pout when they can't go skiing because their child is sick.** I don't believe this one requires elaboration.

- **Wonderful mothers find a heartfelt lesson and a heartfelt way to deliver said lesson when their children encounter failure or disappointment.** I'm pretty successful with this one up to a point. After that point, however, if the child in question is having trouble getting past the problem, the "patience" issue creeps in and I start fantasizing about playing the "You know, when I was a kid" card, which of course I swore I'd never do. So instead I find a semi-gentle way to say, "Suck it up, kid. You've basically got a great life. Get over it."

- **Wonderful mothers kiss boo-boos away.** Again, generally I do not struggle with this, unless they're doing something — for instance, chasing each other around the island in the kitchen in their socks, on the tiled floor — that practically begs for a wipeout, and in that case the boo-boo kissing is usually preceded by a "So, how did that feel?" But then I kiss.

My list could go on, but the point has been made. Based on the June Cleaver Wonderful Mother model, it would seem that

I don't make the grade. But when I think back to the pride I felt for my son that day in karate, I have to believe there's more to it. There's respect, and trust, and sharing, and the drive to help them learn how to be healthy and happy. And, of course, there's love. There's always the love, which to this day is more profound than I could ever have imagined. Maybe, when all is said and done, that's all it takes.

And if it is, then thank you, Sherry. Yes. I really am a wonderful mother.

—m—

Something New Every Day

I'M NOT THE COMPETITIVE SORT. I don't need to win to enjoy a game. I never even played sports as a kid, although there was probably a little competition between my siblings and me in terms of who was smarter. All I know is more than one family Scrabble game came to a crashing halt when someone's tiles became projectiles. For the record, I'm sure the culprit was my younger brother, and my family's stubborn insistence that it was me simply demonstrates the lengths they will all go to win.

But, overall, I'm not competitive. At least, I thought not. Then I went to my daughter's first little indoor basketball scrimmage.

"HONEY, BASKETBALL IS A MOVING GAME!" I called to her. "LEAVE YOUR HAIR ALONE AND COVER YOUR GUY!"

I then clamped my hand over my mouth. Oh my God, I thought; I'm a yeller. I was mortified. I turned to the woman next to me, who had not been yelling at her child, for absolution.

"Hey, did you hear that?" I said nervously. "I've become That Mom, the one who yells at her child from the sidelines! Ha ha ha...oh well! Um, what was your name? Can we be friends?" I clearly needed to be forgiven.

She edged over a bit, silently willing the parent on her other side to move down.

But it was OK, I decided. So I'm a yeller. I'd recognized the behavior, and that was half the battle. It's not like I was demeaning my child or screaming at the coach, for God's sake. I was just offering a little advice, a little guidance that would benefit her play. I was just trying to help.

"OK, BABY, JUST LEAVE THE JERSEY ALONE! PLEASE! WATCH THE BALL! GO! GO! GO!"

I then dropped my head into the coat that was resting in my lap. Somebody help me, I silently pleaded into the faux fur. Stop me before I yell again. I spent the rest of game that way, hoping people would just assume I was napping.

Apparently I didn't realize how competitive I am until the kids were old enough to compete. I mean, sure, my husband almost blew his rapturous future with me when I lost to him bowling on our first date, but that was years ago — surely I've grown since then! Isn't having children supposed to quell that competitive streak?

Of course it does. When playing Go Fish in the early days, I even let the kids win from time to time, because that's what a mother does — and really, parenthetically, where's the fun in beating a toddler? I will admit I shouldn't have so thoroughly enjoyed the Scrabble beat-down I gave a nephew a few years ago, but he was in high school, darn it, and should have known those words. Being an English-teaching writer is not necessarily an advantage, you know.

But if I suspected this isn't healthy mother behavior, ping pong confirmed it.

It started innocently when a neighbor gave us his table. "Oh, come on!" I cheered to my husband. "It'll be fun! I haven't played since I was a child!" I left out the part about marathon rounds in a freezing cold, dark stone basement, my brothers and I all refusing to end on a loss. Maybe I'd blocked it out.

As soon as the table was set up, however, I was 12, and every competitor was a brother. I always complimented a nice opposing shot, but the effect was dampened by the "BOO YEAs!" that followed my own. Both children, at separate times, stopped play to inform me that my celebrating was making them feel bad. My husband was not fazed simply because he kept winning. He was the worst brother of all.

So I've learned something about myself. Even though I model good sportsmanship, my competitiveness might make my cheering sound critical to my kids. Even yelling "You can do it!" could be dismaying if it's yelled with a competitive edge. So I will learn to cheer and appreciate the game for the game's sake. I know I can. Eventually.

But not today. Today my husband is approaching with that telltale glint in his eye, and I'm ready. "Oh yeah?" I taunt. "You talkin' to me? You want a piece of me? Come on, paddle boy. Loser buys dinner!"

—m—

"YOU CAN HAVE TURKEY ANY DAY of the year," I assured my doubting child.

"Is Grandma Barbie coming?" he asked, nervously.

"No," I frostily replied. There was an urgency in his voice that was beginning to irritate me. "Grandma Barbie is not coming. Mommy is perfectly capable of cooking a turkey, thank you."

I mean, really. Grief from a 6-year-old? Yes, it was my first, but I believe I'd watched the process enough to have the general hang of it. My only immediate concern was how to defrost a 14-pound turkey so as to eat it, say, tonight, ultimately deciding to cook it the *next* night.

"That's some turkey," my husband observed as it dropped onto the counter. "What you're doing is probably smart. Take it out now, it'll be thawed by Thanksgiving."

"TURKEYS ARE NOT JUST FOR THANKSGIVING," I bellowed. "That's like saying ham is only for Easter, or pasta is only for Sundays!" My son then left the kitchen in search of intelligent life, offering in his wake, "Mom, pasta *is* only for Sundays. And Monday is Chinese."

"Oh...my...GOD!" I cried. "What is UP with you two? Food is food! It can be eaten any time of day, any day of the year! Now go away, both of you. It's Saturday. I have a pizza to order."

The next day dawned with a fully thawed turkey. By midday I'd assembled everything I needed and went to work I removed the beast from the wrapper, found the dreaded flap, took out the package, placed the turkey in a cooking bag, and put it in the oven.

Two hours and one anxiety attack later, I was on the phone with my mother. "I would just like to know how I was supposed to get the neck out when those legs were tied up like that! It might as well have had a "Keep Out" sign posted across it!"

Silence for a moment, and then, "I gather you forgot to take out the neck?"

"No, I didn't forget!" I cried. "It didn't want to come out! Those legs were practically welded together! I thought that meant that whatever was in there, was supposed to stay in there!"

"Honey," she replied gently, "did you truly never watch me prepare a turkey? You take out the gizzards, and you take out the neck. That's what you do."

"But I thought they were supposed to be in the same place!"

"So what did you think when you pulled out the package and there was no neck there? That you just happened upon a neckless turkey?"

"Well," I said, "it could happen. They could've just chopped this one a little closer to the —"

"OK, OK," she said. "I get the imagery. Just so you're clear on this, though, let's assume from now on that EVERY TURKEY you buy is going to come with a neck. So how is it otherwise?"

"Um, not so good," I said. "I thought maybe my meat thermometer was on the blink or something, but it turns out the meat's really just not done. Which I can't believe, by the way, since I cooked it for almost two full hours. Anyway, I sliced it and put it in the microwave, which apparently was yet another mistake because now it feels and tastes a little like, well, rubber."

"Two hours?" she asked. "You cooked a 14-pound turkey for two hours? Honey, it's 20 minutes per pound, not per year of your son's life! It should've cooked for almost five hours! You're not going to make them eat it, are you?"

I pictured the emergency room scene, complete with social worker and police investigation. "So let me get this straight, ma'am. You fed your family — the people you love most — an undercooked turkey from which you didn't remove the neck, and which you defrosted on the counter for two days, essentially guaranteeing the presence of salmonella?"

"No, of course not," I said to my mom. "I'll make some pasta. After all, it *is* Sunday."

—◊—

I'M AN OLDER MOM. By virtue of that status, I feel I have a duty to set an example for my younger friends, who look to me for advice and wisdom that can only come from the extra years of life experience I possess.

There is one area, however, in which my age may actually be working against me, no matter how hard I try. The area, of course, is s-e-x-u-a-l-i-t-y. In this regard, I'm probably not the perfect role model.

Don't get me wrong; I *want* to be a hip, with-it mom. I'm all about communication and openness and honesty. I want my children to feel comfortable asking me anything, knowing they'll get the unadulterated truth. But the truth is, I don't want them to ask me about this.

In fact, I didn't learn about such things until I was 12, and that was only because my mother was having a baby and thought the subject might come up. Absent my little brother, I'd probably still be in the dark.

In my defense, then, I don't come from a particularly progressive generation in terms of the human body. I shook my b-o-o-t-y for an entire decade without knowing what it meant. My daughter not only knows what it means, she's been shaking it since birth. So I guess I shouldn't have been surprised at our recent conversation, and yet, I was.

I had tucked my beloved into bed and watched her go to sleep. She's so young, so innocent, I thought, so blissfully free of life's conflicts and challenges. Then I noticed her little shoulders start to shake and heard little, kitten-like mews that were rapidly turning into heart-wrenching sobs.

"Honey, what's wrong?" I said as I gently took her in my arms. I envisioned the possibilities — a little friend might have hurt her feelings, or maybe she misses her grandparents. Isn't that sweet, I thought. My little angel wants to see -

"I don't want to have a baby!" she wailed. "They cut you in half to get it out!"

I was stunned. This obviously was not what I was expecting to hear. I took a deep breath, looked up toward the heavens and whispered, "ARE YOU KIDDING ME?"

I then turned back to the case at hand. "Well, first of all, honey, you don't have to have a baby if you don't want to. Second of all, yes, sometimes they have to make a little cut in your tummy to get the baby out, but most times they don't. Thirdly, you don't really need to think about this at your age, OK?"

She was not soothed.

"But when do I tell God I don't want one? What if he gives me a baby in kin-ter-gar-ten?"

There must be a way of talking about this without actually talking about this, I reasoned. She is certainly not emotionally ready, nor does she understand her body yet. Oh, sure, I've noticed subtle signs of burgeoning curiosity; some dancing in front of the mirror, a little body contortion to study her b-o-t-t-o-m, but hey — who doesn't do that, right?

Does that mean I have to give a full-blown explanation before she's even riding the bus? I think not.

And so I said, "You won't have a baby in kindergarten. Now, let's talk about the papier-mache elephant you're making at pre-school!"

"OK," she sniffed. "It's gray. How does the baby come out if they don't cut it out?"

I hesitated, torn between the kind of mother I want to be and the kind I actually am. But it was really no contest.

"Honey, you know what? Mommy's having a hot flash right now. I'm sure it will be over in, oh, 10, 12 years, and then we'll talk about this again, OK? It'll be so much easier — you'll be older, and able to understand more. And of course," I finished happily, "by then you'll know how to s-p-e-l-l!"

—⁓—

I KEEP MY CLEANING SUPPLIES LOCKED in a cabinet under the kitchen sink. I thought that keeping them hidden would protect my kids; if I showed them where and what they were, they'd be more inclined to want to experiment with them and get hurt. If they didn't know the stuff was there, then there wouldn't be any danger.

Of all people, I should know that pretending something doesn't exist doesn't make it so.

My son and I were reading a book together. It was one that might have been a little mature for some 7-year-olds, but we've been reading novels for so long already that I didn't give it a second thought. As we got further into the book, I realized one of the main characters had a drinking problem, although it was never addressed directly.

It wasn't, at least, until the last chapter, when it *was* addressed directly. It became clear then that the character's alcoholism was the central issue behind his actions, and his actions were the central issue of the story.

My son asked me what it meant, and I explained it the best I could on short notice. I told him that some people have a physical problem with alcohol, while others don't, and that people with this problem have a very hard time not drinking, but that not drinking is the only way to be OK. Unfortunately some people aren't able to quit, and it can affect their lives — and the lives of people they love — in a bad way.

He responded, "Alcoholics must be bad people then."

And there it was. I was blindsided. I always knew we would have this conversation one day, because from the generations of alcoholics before me, I am keenly aware of the damage that comes from not talking about it. But I thought he'd be a little older — and that I'd be a little more prepared.

"Oh, no, honey," I said, "Alcoholics aren't bad people. It's a disease, and people with this disease just have to make sure they don't drink."

"But the guy in the book did bad things," he persisted.

"Maybe," I said, "but he was not a bad *person*." I was stalling, trying to put off the inevitable as long as I could. But I simply could not let him walk away from this conversation with the very belief system I wanted to dispel. I could not perpetuate the cycle of guilt and shame of which I'd been a victim all of my life.

"You know," I then said, "Mommy's an alcoholic."

His face took on a look of confusion and fright. "But...are you sick?" he asked.

"No, sweetie, I'm not sick. I've been sober for 15 years. I'm what they call a 'recovering alcoholic.' I was able to get help a long time ago, before you were born, before I even met Daddy. I knew I had to get better if I ever wanted to have you all in my life someday."

He mulled this over for a few moments and matter-of-factly asked, "Will I be an alcoholic?"

Once again I was not prepared for the question. The truth is that, based on my family history, there's a chance he may have a problem with drinking — but he's certainly too young to adopt that worry. Still I chose not to lie...a choice that was more difficult than I care to admit.

"I don't know," I finally said, "but I do know that whatever challenges you face when you get older, Daddy and I will help you through them. That's why we talk about things, so that you'll always be able to come to us." That satisfied him, and I thought it was the end of it.

It wasn't. He came home from school a few days later, put down his backpack, and said, "Hi, Mom! Um...you were drunk, weren't you?"

Wiping the initial shock off my face, I replied, "Well, yes, I guess I was...I mean, well — why do you ask, honey?"

He pulled out a paper from school that explained the workings of the lungs, with a section on the ill effects of smoking.

"The teacher said that we shouldn't smoke, because it's addictive and once you start sometimes you can't stop. And I raised my hand and said, 'That's like my mom with drinking!'" He was so proud of himself for making that connection, and yet in need of some reassurance that it was OK to do so.

I stood there silently, trying to picture his classmates' dinner conversations that night. I was imagining his party invitations drying up and play dates dwindling away when suddenly I caught myself. I was doing exactly what I did when I was a kid, exactly what I didn't want my kids to do. I was letting myself be ashamed.

And in that moment, with my son waiting expectantly for some clue that he hadn't done anything wrong, I knew what I had to say and I knew I had to be ready to live it. I kissed his head and said, "Yes, honey. That's right. They're very similar." He smiled and walked away, presumably filing the information away in his head under "Things to Know Later." And he taught me something in the process.

The mere existence of something does not make it dangerous. What makes it dangerous is not understanding what it is and what it can do, which leads to judgment and fear and prejudice. Knowledge, I'm learning, truly is power, and so I'm going to get my children and head for the kitchen.

We've got some cabinets to unlock.

—⚬⚬—

WHEN I WAS A KID, life was easier. There weren't as many rules, there weren't as many toys, and there weren't as many TV stations. Houses were essentially places to eat, sleep, and, when necessary, bathe. And since parents back then were not nearly as interested as we are today in their children's amusement, weekends found us essentially gone after breakfast with the lone directive of my generation — "Be home by dark."

And we not only survived, I think we were stronger for it.

For better or worse, things are a little different these days. We have a house that's made for kids. There's plenty of room to play inside, and the kids' bedrooms are decorated just the way they want them. The play room, painted in primary colors with a chalkboard wall, is packed with toys of every kind. And there is a beautiful, park-like back yard complete with wooden swingset and oversized sandbox.

The world is also a little scarier today, and so when it comes to amusing the kids, parents such as myself are a little more reluctant to leave children to their own devices. I admit to some guilt in this area, and I sheepishly watch my mother roll her eyes as I begin my 34th straight game of Trouble.

But that's the way it is. I have never been comfortable sending my children out to play for 12 hours at a time. So when I suggested to said kids that they invite their twin friends over one day, I was more than a little surprised at their response.

"Um, can we go there instead?" my son the diplomat asked. "Nothing personal, Mom." His sister stood behind him, enthusiastically nodding her support. "Yeah, nuttin' personable."

I didn't understand this mutiny, and so my son felt obliged to explain. Instead of the pointer and chalkboard he usually needs to teach me something, however, his tool of choice was a tape recorder that apparently his father had given him. Whether his father knew there was a tape in it remains to be seen.

My son looked at me guiltily as he turned the tape recorder to "play." Suddenly I heard my own voice.

"Sneakers off when you come in, please. No running in the house, please. No throwing the soccer ball in the house. No hitting each other with swords. No running! No climbing on the bunk bed. No drinks in the family room. Please leave the cushions on the couch. We draw on paper, not furniture, please. Don't put the marker in your mouth. And for the love of God, would you stop running in the house!

"Put on sunscreen. Put on bug spray. Stay in the back yard. Don't walk on Daddy's new grass. Sneakers off in the sandbox, please. And take the leaves out before you play in there. Yes, take the bugs out, too. No throwing sand. No hitting. No throwing the ball at someone's head. All right, no throwing ANYTHING at anyone's head. Don't come down the slide face first."

"No bikes in the backyard, please. Don't hit. Don't play in the leaves until you make sure there are no sticks or dog poop in there. No using karate on friends. No using sticks as weapons. Wear your helmets with scooters. PLEASE stay in the back yard. And PLEASE DON'T HIT!"

"OK, you know what? Everybody inside. Rest time. Quiet time for 30 minutes. And no TV!"

As I listened to the monologue, I was at once impressed with my son's grasp of technology and shocked at the high pitch of my voice. And shocked, as well, at my litany of rules.

My son, in his own sweet and wise-beyond-his-years way, had his own theory as to why I am Manic Mommy and his friends' mom is not. "It's not that she doesn't have any rules," he said. "She just doesn't have as many of them. Maybe it's because she has three kids and you only have two. Maybe she's just too busy to think about them."

Ouch, I thought. Did my son just tell me I have too much time on my hands?

"And don't forget, she's a lot younger than you. Maybe she just doesn't get as...um...well...*nutso* about things."

Ooh, double-ouch. Now I'm OLD with too much time on my hands.

"Well, OK, fine," I sniffed, trying to mask my hurt with mere indignation. "I'll take you down to your friends' house. I don't mind. I have things to do anyway. But remember to be polite and respectful, and use your good manners. Don't eat junk food. Say 'please' and 'thank you.' Share the toys, and play nicely together."

"And oh, yeah — be home by dark!"

—∿∿—

IF YOU'VE EVER TAKEN A DOG for training, one thing becomes immediately clear. The classes aren't for training the dog — they're for training you. You need to understand the way a dog thinks before you can begin to understand how to peacefully coexist with him. The goal isn't to break the dog's spirit so that he'll do what you want; it's to understand the dog's spirit and use that knowledge to help him be safe and happy.

Anyone who's ever had children knows that children are not dogs. But I'm learning that the lesson is almost the same.

I was once quietly and guiltily confiding in a friend about my daughter's maniacal aversion to hairbrushes, headbands and barrettes. Coupled with her equally headstrong determination to grow her hair long, we have been reduced to shouting matches more often than I care to admit.

"All of a sudden," I told my friend of this latest incident, "it was like we were BOTH 5 years old, and I was yelling at her that I was going to make an appointment to cut her hair off. That's when I realized I was at the end of my rope and had to walk away."

My friend didn't bat an eye. "I have the best conditioner — I use it on my older daughter's hair or we can't get a comb through it. And they make tug-proof hair bands, too!" These things didn't occur to me because I've always had short, fine hair. My friend has beautiful, thick hair…like my daughter. My Achille's heel with my child caused my friend no grief at all.

"Now, my son — *he* makes me crazy!" she said, laughing.

My relief was palpable — not just from a possible solution to the hair problem, but because she admitted to having a challenging child of her own. The guilt I'd felt over this most recent meltdown was unnerving, particularly because I don't think I've ever felt it with my older child. I've never had such a meltdown with him. He simply is not that combination of mercurial, stubborn, and 5.

Why do I feel so guilty? Because I get frustrated — when she doesn't take "no" for an answer, when the toes of her socks have to fit just right, when she wants to wear shorts in the winter and arrange 30 dolls just so before bed. While I'm learning to choose my battles, I get frustrated at my own lack of patience, and I feel guilty because it makes it seem as though I love my challenging child less.

Kids from the beginning of time have accused parents of playing favorites, of loving one child more than another, of treating siblings unfairly. Parents from the beginning of time have lived with the guilt of not loving each child the same. But each child is NOT the same. They're different. Is it possible to love your children equally but differently? I think it is.

I love them both more than life — my son, who has always been empathic, sensitive, helpful, loving, and only occasionally stubbornly perfectionist, and my daughter, who has always been moody, argumentative, dramatic, strong-willed, stubborn, and only occasionally affectionate. I didn't know kids could be that different from each other, especially in the same family... although puppies and wolves are in the same family too.

My daughter is more independent, imaginative, creative, focused and clever than I will ever be. Every single element of her personality that now leads us to trouble is just what I wanted her to have as an adult. I don't want to quash them, or dim them, or stifle them. I just need to be able to handle them at this time in her life, and that's not always easy...which is perhaps the understatement of the year.

Certainly, it's not all battles and meltdowns. When she's not making me crazy, she's making me laugh. And the occasional hug or unsolicited "I love you, Mommy" have become touching beyond belief, because I know that affection is difficult for her. It doesn't mean she doesn't love me. It means we're different, and I need to learn to appreciate those differences so that I can be as good a mother to her as I am to my son...the "easy" one.

My "easy child" is like me. I instinctively understand him, how he thinks. I can predict how he will react in any given situation and plan accordingly. There are few meltdowns, few acts of overt disobedience, few gray areas of acceptable behavior. We "get" each other because we're similar.

My "difficult child" isn't challenging because of who she is. She's challenging because of who I am. I don't always understand her, or how she thinks, or why she reacts the way she does. I'm also probably a little jealous of her confidence and her unshakable belief in her decisions. Of one thing, however, I am certain: All of these traits are what make her unique and exceptional. I just need to learn how to teach her to use them to be safe and happy.

Fortunately, it's an ongoing class. And as I tell us both almost every day, don't worry. Mommy's signing back up.

—⁂—

MY DAUGHTER WAS NAGGING — er, persistently requesting something recently, and in a fit of exasperation I said, "We'll see." She walked away doing the little fist-pump "Yes!" thing as though scoring a victory. And I thought, oh, isn't that cute? She still thinks that means "you might have a shot," rather than "I know if I say this you will leave me in peace." How sweet!

And I don't mean to be a cruel mommy, either. I do think her innocence is adorable. I'm also keenly aware that it's going to last about another week. After all, she has a big brother who's been there and done that, and it's getting more and more challenging for him to keep his enlightenment to himself.

I've therefore taken it upon myself to produce this for the children, a "parent-to-English dictionary" of sorts. My hope is that if I come clean with this stuff now, the kids will remember my generosity and provide a similar "teen-to-English" version when the time comes. And yes, I'll let you know how that works for me.

So, children, let's start with the basics. When I say to you, "Don't make me come in there," it means, I'm coming in there. Not this second, maybe, because I'm either napping or busy but, rest assured, I'm coming in there. So knock it off.

"My patience is wearing thin" really means my patience was gone about five minutes ago and my head is going to physically blow off my shoulders if you don't stop doing what you're doing or start doing what you're being told to do.

"Am I talking to myself here?" You guys really seem to love this one, often responding with a resounding "Yes!" But of course I know I'm not talking to myself. It's called a rhetorical question. What it means is, "Somebody in this house had better start listening to me, and it had better not just be the dog."

"Every day is children's day" admittedly used to bother me as much as it bothers you, but you'll understand when you have kids of your own. For now, you'll just have to trust me on this one. It means that Mommy is treated special one day a year; you are treated special every single flippin' day of your lives.

"If you don't stop crying, I'm going to give you something to cry about!" Let me start this one by saying yes, I get it. You already had something to cry about or you wouldn't be crying. What I mean is, I don't think what you're crying about is worth crying about, and if you don't stop, then you'll have something worthwhile to be crying about. Make sense?

"Pick up your room." This is another one that you people seem to get a kick out of. Yes, I'm aware you can't actually pick up your room. It'd be too heavy. What I mean is PICK THE STUFF UP OFF THE FLOOR, before everything you own becomes a chew toy.

"Stop it" — and this is one of my favorites — means stop it now. Not in two minutes, not in 10 minutes, not in an hour. Stop. It. Now. (Also applies to "Go to bed," "Turn that down," and "Do your homework.")

Last but not least, no, I don't actually have eyes in the back of my head. What this means is that mommies pretty much know everything you do. We're all-seeing. There is no escaping us. It's designed to entice you to behave yourselves. See how all this works? Awesome. Lesson over.

In the meantime, my son wants to know if I'm going to discuss things parents say that children think are really just kind of, in his words, "stupid." A particular pet peeve of the younger set is the old "Because I said so" philosophy, which evidently intelligent children everywhere find ridiculous if not completely weenie-ish.

So he has a point. Parents say some pretty silly things

sometimes, from a kid's perspective. Are they deserving of air time, so to speak? Worthy of ink? Will I break down and give children everywhere the satisfaction of admitted parental imperfection, all in the hope that my kids might possibly talk to me in another decade? Hmmmmm.

We'll see.

—⚏—

THE BIG YELLOW BUS IS ONCE MORE rumbling down our street, signaling the end of summer and the beginning of another chapter in my life. My youngest is now in kindergarten. Big brother and little sister stand together at the bus stop, he surreptitiously looking out for her, his fear for her safety and feelings only slightly stronger than his fear of being caught caring.

I stand here and think of all the emotions I should be feeling, that any normal mother would be feeling at this momentous occasion in her children's life — a deep sense of pride, hope for the future, nostalgia for baby days long gone, and maybe even a little fear about what lies in store for these innocent young people. I should be crying.

So why, then, am I doing The Happy Dance in my driveway as the bus is pulling away?

A friend once told me of this phenomena. She spoke wistfully of a sort of unbridled joy that springs forth as the bus pulls out of sight on that first September school day, causing her to literally break out in an uncensored demonstration of bodily movement.

At the conclusion of said display, she sends around her annual e-mail congratulating us all for surviving another summer, and encouraging us to locate what's left of our sanity and rejoin civilization.

I've always read these e-mails with mixed emotions; happy to be included in the group, and yet somehow sad for these parents who are overjoyed to be sending their children back to school. I always thought I should just be cc'd, rather than directly addressed, because the e-mail didn't quite speak to my situation.

It's too bad, really, I would think to myself as the dancing emoticons skipped across my computer screen. I must have the most extraordinary children, because I've felt nothing but sorrow these last few years as they went first to preschool, and then pre-k, and now elementary school. In fact, I cried each time.

So color me surprised when I started dancing the jig with the other parents on the street as the bus pulled away. I didn't even know that I *knew* the jig.

And I find it somewhat troubling, I don't mind saying — not that I know the jig, which is an entirely separate issue, but that I'm so happy to send them off to school. I used to ask my son, "Gosh, sweetie, I love you so much; what will I do when you're in school for the next 12 years?" To which he always sweetly replied, "You'll sleep, Mom."

I would sigh and think, he's so smart. But having my kids in school, I also thought, will nevertheless be a sad, lonely time for me. Oh, sure, I might grab a nap here and there, but I wouldn't be happy about it — and I certainly wouldn't be *celebrating* it. No, sending my kids to school was going to be a devastating transition in my life.

And it was, really...for about seven seconds. That's when I realized that I was a mother like any other, with wonderful children who, when they're home, necessarily take up 100 percent of my time. And to the applause of the other parents present, I joined in the dance.

I don't know why I resisted so much. Maybe I thought that by needing time for me, I was somehow negating my love for my children. After all, I had two healthy, wonderful kids relatively late in life, with no complications — how dare I need some alone time! I should appreciate what I have and show that appreciation by spending every waking moment with them!

This begs the questions, then: Am I supposed to feel guilty for wanting my kids back in school? Does it make me less of a mother, somehow, that I miss my alone time, my cleaning time, my writing time? Am I saying to all the world that I don't love my kids because I can hear the school bus approach from a block away like other mothers can hear their babies cry in another part of the house?

No, no, and no, if you were looking for the answers there. I love my kids just fine, thank you. And I am able to show them that I love them much more easily when I'm relaxed, sane, and yes, napped.

Looking around at other parents, I'm realizing that it's OK to need some space. In fact, I bet it's healthy. You show me a parent who can give his or her all, 100 percent of the time, and I'll show you a parent who's about one shrieking child away from an extended mommy or daddy time-out. And that's not good for anybody, let alone our kids.

Yes, it's September once again, and as my youngest joins the neighborhood kids at the steps of the big yellow bus, I will join, finally, the generations of parents who have come before me, parents who have paid their dues and arrived, guilt-free and without fear, at this driveway where I now stand.

Parents who, at this moment, are busily waving their arms and moving their feet to the immortal words of the Bee Gees, who said we should, in fact, be dancing.

—∽∾—

OUR TEEN-AGE NEIGHBOR CAME OVER recently to visit our new puppy. We've known her for several years, and she's blossomed into a beautiful young lady — a big girl, to my daughter. My daughter silently walked over to her, arms outstretched, and hugged her around the waist.

Our neighbor was clearly befuddled, as my daughter is not typically a hugger. In fact, I can count on one hand the number of hugs she has given me in her lifetime, and one was out of fear of falling into the toilet when she was 2 and so it probably doesn't count. However, I'd been seeing the same behavior toward bigger girls all summer long, usually accompanied by a suspicious sideways glance in my direction.

"I'm beginning to think my mother's kind of a doofus," said the hug, "and I want to be like you."

She is the oft-hailed 6-years-old-going-on-16. Certainly I'd heard of the phenomenon, but apparently assumed my parenting skills were such that I'd be exempt. All I had to do was shelter my daughter from the outside world for a decade or so; encourage My Little Ponies and "Dora the Explorer" and pretend Bratz and "Hannah Montana" aren't available here. How hard could it be? Right?

Of course not right.

We went to a graduation party this summer that included

many teen-agers. When it came time to leave, I found my daughter in the game room, surrounded by a half-circle of older girls. She was gazing adoringly at them, and they were smiling down on her and chatting. If I didn't know better, I'd have sworn she was taking a class on teenage-girl-ness.

I shouldn't have been surprised. My daughter has always been in a hurry to grow up. When she was 2, she had her first crush (on my husband's trainer), and I knew we were in trouble. At 4 she asked if I could get her some breasts at the store. At 6 she was wearing sports bras and bikinis. And always, always, she watched the older girls, wherever she could find them. Watched, and then hugged.

My girl starts first grade this month, marking her first year in all-day school. Unfortunately, because of where her birthday falls, she had three years of half-day preschool, and because of where we live, she had half-day kindergarten. Also unfortunately, she's been ready for all-day school since she left the womb. It's finally happening, and she couldn't be more excited. And I couldn't be more afraid.

There will be older girls everywhere — in the halls, in the lunchroom, on the playground — girls from whom she will learn, she thinks, all of the life lessons that Mommy is so intent on denying her. She will study how they dress, how they talk, how they act around boys, how they act with each other. She will memorize the kinds of school supplies and lunch boxes they use, the shoes they wear, the backpacks they carry.

She will try to wear her hair like theirs and imitate their nail polish and lip gloss. She will adopt their language, their style, their attitudes. She's going to watch them on the bus, observe their interactions, listen to their conversations, and try to take in their very aura. And I'm beginning to see that there's not much I can do about it.

It's not that I'm obsolete, I know. I'll still be in charge of where she is at all times, what clothes she owns, who she hangs with after school, what she watches on television, and the video games she plays, but I have to admit that right now, those things don't seem as important as what the older girls are in charge of.

For all intents and purposes, older girls are in charge of my baby's soul for the next few years, until she starts believing that her own judgments are good enough and her own style is good enough and her own looks are good enough and her own life is good enough.

And they can help her with all of that, if they will try. I'm praying that the girls my daughter meets are happy, healthy, emotionally and physically strong, independent, kind, empathic and generous. I'm praying that she will meet girls like this, girls like herself, who will convince her through their own being that herself is a great person to be.

So this one's for the girls. Please be good to mine as I send her off to first grade; be kind to her, and protect her, and remember that you were once down there looking up. Be aware that she's listening to every word you say, and watching everything you do, and that you have the power to influence her self-esteem in ways that I simply can't.

And if she comes up and wraps her arms around you, please hug her back, and maybe remind her that doofus though she may be, her mommy loves her...no matter how big she gets.

—⁂—

Mental Pause

THE PURPOSE OF A VACATION, they say, is to make us
feel better. It is an opportunity to escape from real life
for awhile, to pamper ourselves, to do things we ordinarily
don't do. It is meant to restore our mental health so that the
usual daily routine isn't so bad. That's why we look forward to
it each and every year.

This year, with the kids a little bit older, we had a family
meeting to discuss where to go. After some debate and discussion, we decided as a family to go to the ocean. After making
said decision, the husband and children then went about their
lives, their jobs apparently complete.

As most people know, the continental U.S. is surrounded
on three sides by various oceans. Time of year also had to be
considered, as well as hurricane and/or breeding horseshoe
crab seasons. Amount of travel time was factored in, including whether to travel by plane, train or automobile. Airline

and train prices were examined and compared, specials investigated, and routes experimented with. Amount of allotted vacation time was also considered, as well as the children's various sports camps and pre-planned summer activities.

After many late nights and hours on various vacation web sites, I found an area that was met with roars of applause, and I therefore began looking for accommodations. I went on the internet and starting searching for places that seemed to encompass the various familial criteria, having made the monumental mistake of seeking their input. For example, our beach needed to be within one day's driving because we didn't want to spend the whole time traveling. It had to have good shells, and the cottage needed to be decent; no shacks, and no bugs, particularly spiders. The cottage needed to fall within a certain price range, and it needed to be right on the beach — but not so close that we'd get knocked out by a rogue wave or that the kids could wander into the ocean in a sleepwalking state. It needed to be near a town so we would have activities and restaurants and stuff to do on rainy days. But if we could find a place where it doesn't rain, they all agreed, that'd be perfect.

After many more late nights and long hours on the computer, I narrowed our choices to three places, and put them before the group. They unanimously chose a cottage and I thought, excellent! Get my Staples button, because that was easy! The husband and children then disbanded and went about their lives, their job, again, complete. I booked the cottage.

As vacation time neared, preparations began. I bought window shades for the car so the kids' handheld games would be viewable, and a splitter and headphones for the DVD player in the car so they could watch their movies without the husband and I having to listen along. I bought little neck pillows for their little necks so that when they fell asleep in the car, the top half of their bodies did not end up prone in the middle seat. I returned our books — early! — to the library, went to the post office to stop the mail, and to the grocery store to get snacks for the ride.

I made arrangements for care of the cat and watering of the landscaping, including having spare keys made and disbursed. I Mapquested directions for the trip there and the trip back, including researching major construction areas and anticipated delays. I gathered all necessary chargers for cell phones, cameras, Nintendos, Game Boys and DVD players. I also took votes and collected movies for the trip.

The next step involved beach basics: sunscreen, hats, towels, beach umbrella, coolers, beach chairs. Then there were sweatshirts for the kids and me, as well as extra pillows and the requisite stuffed animals and special blankets. Next came boogie boards, swim fins, inflatable rings, shovels, pails and swim shoes. Along with the swim shoes went flip-flops, sandals and sneakers. Footwear: check.

The rest of the packing followed several loads of laundry, ensuring that each traveler had every available outfit at his or her disposal. This portion included, for the boy, the girl and the mother, the following: bathing suits, underwear, socks, pajamas (including a variety of both nightgowns and boxer/top combos), shirts, shorts, skorts, sundresses, and Yankees T-shirts (all of them). This was followed by what I like to call "The Bathroom Bag," which includes everything from toothbrushes and toothpaste to Band-Aids to Children's Tylenol and Benadryl. It also includes hairbrushes, combs, shampoos, conditioners, detanglers, mousses and gels, and other requisite shower products.

The morning of our departure finally arrived. I got both kids up at 6 a.m. and went about getting their breakfasts, making coffee, filling the cooler, and feeding the cat. I was organizing and assembling maps, directions, sightseeing brochures and pamphlets into neat piles when my husband came downstairs, freshly showered and shaved, carrying a duffel bag.

"Hey," he said, "I'm all packed — what's going on here? Aren't you guys ready?!"

I glanced at this man to whom I've pledged my life. My attention then returned to the pile of travel books in front of me, finally resting on the AAA guide. It was a good book, a useful book. I had perused it often in the previous weeks searching for just the right places to eat, just the right things to do. It was my travel Bible, the book that calmed me and guided me through the entire planning process. I gently removed it from the stack and hurled it at him.

His surprised and somewhat indignant look as he barely sidestepped to safety assured me that he understood my point, and I couldn't help thinking, well, what do you know? It's just like they said about vacations — I really do feel better!

—∽—

THE BOY CAME INTO THE FAMILY ROOM recently and announced, "Hey, it's dinnertime. Where are we going?"

"Chinese!" the girl chimed in. "I want Chinese!"

"We were there twice this week," the husband reminded her. "Let's go someplace different. How about Mexican?"

"No, not good for me," replied the boy. "Pasta?"

"Not in the mood," said the husband.

"Hey, I thought I might cook tonight," I interrupted. "I have chicken in the fridge, and I could make a salad and potatoes!"

There was silence as they all momentarily appraised me.

"How about that new steak place?" said the boy, turning his attention back to the group. "I could do steak tonight."

"I don't want steak!" cried the girl. "I want dumplings! Chinese dumplings!"

"Nah," said the husband. "How about Thai?"

In the car on the way to the restaurant, I was uncharacteristically quiet, and the husband asked why.

"Why am I upset?" I cried. "Oh, I don't know; maybe because the biggest decision in our house every day is where to have dinner! Maybe because historically, women had three jobs in life: to cook for their family, to clean the house, and to raise the kids — and I only do one!"

The boy in the back seat said, "Which one?" When I finished screaming and pulled my head back in the window, I informed him that, in fact, I raise the kids.

I don't think I fell far from the tree, if that's a defense. I don't think my mother truly enjoyed cooking. I always had the sense, come dinnertime, that her heart just wasn't into it. She did make wonderful meals for us night after night, but there was always the unspoken question in her eyes as she served us: "Are there really still seven of you?"

I say essentially the same thing every night; "Who are you

people, and why are you looking to me for food?" Unlike my mother, who did not have the same options, I rarely cook. And despite the fact that my kids have never asked, "Mommy, why don't you cook?" I have found myself feeling very guilty about it.

I'm wondering if I'm teaching my children to make choices based on their interests and desires, and then to feel guilty about them.

Guilt is a tough emotion, and one with which I often struggle. I now even find myself feeling guilty for feeling guilty, and I dare you to top that. When I unconsciously use it as a discipline weapon against my children, they know to stop me with a "Guilt alert!" call that helps me to break the pattern. Now I need to learn to stop myself.

I'm not a great cook. I'm not what you'd call a neat freak. I don't sew or knit. I find laundry strangely therapeutic, but generally those other things rank somewhere close to unmedicated root canals in terms of things I really enjoy. I envy people who do them, but I'm simply not one of them. And my children don't care.

They care about the other things, though; I throw a mean football, I pitch to the boy and help the girl with her karate. I teach college and write books and plan absolutely fabulous vacations. I support my husband's business with my lightning-fast typing skills (of which I am strangely proud) and help my children with homework that I can barely understand.

I am the pets' caretaker (including but not limited to buying live crickets for the barking tree frogs) and the buyer of all clothes and most electronics. I am a chauffeur, a secretary, an enthusiastic coach and watcher of all sports. I am things that many mothers of previous generations simply did not have the opportunity to be.

Am I a cook? No. But I do my best to teach my kids to be healthy, eat well, and make intelligent, informed choices based on their interests and desires...whether they be Mexican, Chinese or Thai.

—⟩⟩⟨—

MOTHERS HAVE A BOND. For some of us, it might have started with the act of childbirth, which is beautiful and magical but essentially redefines our sense of dignity and modesty for the rest of our lives. For others it may stem simply from the task of raising children, from the early days of projectile vomiting to the later days of living with teen-agers who think we're complete morons.

Whatever the reason, mothers have a bond.

Don't get me wrong; fathers are cool, too. You know you are. There are more than a few who are quite comfortable buying tampons or whatnot; I've just always gotten the sense that they are as not as interested in talking about these tasks as they may be about performing them. So when it comes down to the real nitty-gritty, I've found that moms have a connection like no other.

This became abundantly clear to me after my recent back surgery. Little did I know that the back pain itself and the embarrassment associated with my 7-year-old tying my shoes would not be the only issues; evidently the pain medicine that gets you moving in some areas also stops you moving in others, if you catch my drift. I was at a loss as to where to turn. Then a friend came over, a mom.

"Well, if the fruits and veggies and stool softeners aren't working," she said without batting an eye, "you may need laxatives — or you might want to try suppositories. I had to use them on my son when he was younger and they worked great. Just make sure you're married to a bathroom!"

This was from another friend, another mom who's also caring for an elderly parent: "I just picked up some fiber powder for my father-in-law. He swears by it — if you can get past the smell!"

Do you see the trend here? We have no secrets. Mothers share shamelessly, because we know there is no shame. Embarrassment, maybe. Shame, no.

And it's a good thing, too, because otherwise we'd all be suffering in silence, wondering if anyone else has ever gone through what we're going through or if we're just really the worst parents that ever lived. Do other people's kids get molluskum? How about lice or plantar warts? And the answer is yes, yes and yes. Of course they do. They get those things and more.

Once we start sharing this kind of thing, it's amazing what comes out. The flood gates are opened over a night of bunko or purse parties or even walking the dog. One woman's eyebrow is higher than the other. Another's left foot is a half-size bigger than the right. Another's afraid that pretty soon her beard is going match her husband's. No, wait, sorry. That one's me.

And then there are the all-time favorites, the pee-your-pants stories. I would argue that a mother has not lived until she has peed her pants in public at least once. To those of you who think you're alone in this one, I suggest getting together with some girlfriends and opening this particular Pandora's box. I would not suggest, however, doing so on a trampoline.

So many of these issues can be sources of shame, if left alone. When shared, however, they return to what they were in the first place — stories of humanness. I've decided that it's not necessarily misery that loves company; it's simply the fact of our being that loves it. Company validates us, and helps us to remember — or maybe even realize for the first time — that we're not alone in our experiences, good or bad. Many others have been there and done that and lived to tell.

So when you need help with something personal or private or just plain embarrassing, find a mom. More often than not, she'll be willing and able to give you the straight, uh, poop.

—⚏—

MY SON WAS UPSET THE OTHER NIGHT because he realized he'd only practiced piano a couple times throughout the week and his lesson was the next day. He was very hard on himself, and I said, "I'm sorry, honey. You're only 9; Mommy needs to remind you more often. That's part of my job."

"But you're in menopause!" he cried. "You can't remember anything!"

And it hit me. I'm not too young for menopause; my *children* are too young for it. Or, rather, for me to be in it. I just finished telling them how a woman's body makes babies, and now I have to tell them how it stops. It's like the short-attention-span-theater version of life talks. Gee, maybe they'll at least be in middle school before I tell them why my bladder's hanging down to my knees.

But I'm not alone. I've met many, many moms my age —
with young children — going through the same thing. Heck,
if they can make a Broadway musical about it, then there's
something going on. And what's going on, quite simply, is that
we're having kids later. At my son's ball games, I could just as
easily be sitting next to a pregnant mom as a fellow hot-flasher.

As one friend says, though, 50 is the new 30, so I'm really only...hmmm...26. I can live with that assessment. I feel
young, and whatever my body has to go through, it will go
through. It's biology, that's all. It's just taking some getting used
to; when my mom went through all this, I'd already finished
college and commiserated with her over some cheese and a nice
Chardonnay — not Lucky Charms and a juice box.

Besides, I've been denying my aging for as long as I can
remember (ha! That's a joke, because of course I CAN'T
REMEMBER!) When the state fair guy guessed my age three
years too high I blamed my husband ("You've got gray hair!
Of course he's going to think I'm older! I told you to wait
over there!")

When the emergency room doctor had trouble quieting my
2-year-old daughter and gave her to me, saying, "Tell Grandma
where it hurts," I blamed the truly poor lighting (and lest you
misread me, there is nothing wrong with being a grandma.
Some of the nicest people I know are grandmas. And I look
forward to being one myself...in 20 years.)

And when the kids ask why I can't jump on the trampoline
with them without peeing my pants, I of course blame them.

But eventually there was no more denial. We were all
walking through Target one day when I started sweating un-
controllably. My hair became soaked, my neck was dripping,

I was shaking and my knees were weak. My husband watched the whole thing in horror, wondering if I was having a heart attack or merely trying to embarrass him. "What the heck's wrong with you?" he asked as I sat on a display to recover.

I glared at him. "It's a hot flash, *dear*," I hissed. "You know, those things that I'm 'not really having'?"

And then there are the one-sided conversations we have after the lights go out.

"Honey, it's too hot in here. Open a window, would you?"

"OK, now I'm kind of chilly. Can you close it back up a little? Thanks, babe."

"Um, sweetie, I'm sweatin' over here. What about that window?"

"OK, am I the only one in here with goosebumps? Close the window, already!"

"IT'S SO HOT MY SHIRT IS SOAKED. PLEASE, HONEY. FOR THE LOVE OF GOD, JUST OPEN THE WINDOW!"

So I have to explain all this to the kids, or else they'll think Mommy is sick. Between the hot flashes, night sweats, irritability, weight gain, mood swings, facial hair, hormonal acne, and memory problems...actually, except for the first two, that all sounds alarmingly normal. No wonder they're confused.

Wait — we have a piano?

—⁓—

WE RECENTLY GOT NEW FURNITURE and carpeting in the family room. I love everything about new stuff — the smell of it, how it almost glows with lack of human contact. It's pristine, pure, perfectly clean. Then the inevitable first spill comes...and I breathe a silent sigh of relief.

The perfect period is over, and now we can go back to living. There's no more tension, no more being extra careful. Perfection, after all, is a pretty high standard to be held to.

That's why I've always loved my children unconditionally, encouraged them unconditionally, and praised them for their efforts regardless of outcome. I've made a point of not expecting them to be perfect. Instead I've taught them to be kind, and fair, and respectful, and helpful. And in an effort to model these values, I've gotten very successful at hiding my own flaws, my own insecurities, my own mistakes. They don't need to see those. They need positive, successful role models, of which I am one.

When I would tuck my son in at night and he'd tell me I was the best mommy in the whole world, I would beam with pride. Yes, I would think, I am doing a good job.

Yet when my children are devastated by a wrong answer on a test, or terrified that I might be angry when they spill a glass of milk, I am completely befuddled. Why do they react like this? I never yell at them for making mistakes, never lose my temper over torn pants or muddy shoes — so why are they so hard on themselves?

The answer finally hit me recently when I swore in front of my daughter, which I can honestly say had not happened until that point. I was mortified. I couldn't apologize enough, and I berated myself for hours. And suddenly I knew where they got it from.

They're perfectionists because of me. Not because of what I say, but because of what I do...or in this case, don't do.

I never let my children see me fail. I never let them see me fall short, or make a mistake, or deal with the consequences of making a mistake or bad judgment. And while I'd love to say that's because it never happens, most people know otherwise. It happens all the time. I just hide it well.

I may not overtly expect perfection, but the mere fact that I never let them see me fail implies it. By modeling "perfect" behavior for my children so that they grow up happy and guilt-free and shame-free, I've created the opposite — an environment where, despite my unconditional love, the need for perfection is omnipresent. And that can only set them up for disappointment, in life and in themselves.

Now I'm facing one of my life's great ironies — my children demanding perfection of themselves because they think they have a perfect mother, which is so far from the truth as to be laughable. So what do I do now? How can I begin to teach my children to love themselves as unconditionally as I love them?

I need to start being me again, I think. I need to show my kids who I am, and let them see me fail once in a while. They think that I don't; I have a box of rejections to show them that proves otherwise. But it also proves that I try. I've always told them to try their best and I'll be happy; now I need to show them how that works.

I need to let them see me struggle, maybe, with my weight or self-esteem issues. By hiding them, I'm showing my kids either that my problems aren't worthwhile, or that they're shameful. What I should be showing them instead is that everyone has issues and they can be dealt with and they're a part of life.

I want to show them my failures and disappointments, and then show them how to recover and move on. How can they learn to let things go if they have no example? I no longer think I need to protect them from disappointments; I merely need to show them it's OK to be disappointed, and to go forward.

And I'm going to show them that I'm human, and flawed, and still completely worthy of love. That no one is perfect, and that's OK, because we can still be great. We can still be smart, and passionate, and sympathetic, and caring, and funny. I'm going to show them that I really AM the best mommy in the world, by gathering them in my arms on our brand new furniture.

And spilling on it.

—⁂—

"WELL, WHEN I WAS A KID..."

I was in physical therapy one day, trapped on my cot with a hot pack on my back, when I heard those dreaded words from an older patient outside my door. Another's grandchild had an early soccer game the next day, and he said, "Well, when I was a kid, I was up every day at 5 a.m. just do to chores! Can you imagine kids today doing that?"

The other man said, "Hey, do you remember the harvest? I'd work for pennies just for the chance to drive the tractor!" It went on like this for several minutes.

I also remember hearing those same words from my parents at the beginning of a story I'd no doubt heard before, which usually involved something about walking to school five miles in the snow, uphill both ways. And my response was always the same, at least in my head: "Yes, I get it. You had it worse."

I knew I must be growing up, then, while listening to these

two guys in therapy, because not only did the conversation not make me cringe, I was enthralled with this snapshot of how it used to be.

It started me thinking about how hard I try not to say those words to my own children, because I don't want to sound like my parents sounded to me. I don't want the words, "Well, I didn't have that when I was a kid, and I turned out OK" to ever leave my lips — mainly because anybody who ever says that deserves the debate that will follow.

I didn't want to believe that I've become that parent. And it made me realize, suddenly, that maybe being that parent isn't so bad.

Every generation wants to make their children's lives better than theirs, give them more opportunities with less hardship. But how arrogant I must have seemed to my own parents all this time to believe that I've gotten it right — that my generation figured it out. How hurt they must have been each time they saw us blatantly doing the opposite of what they did, as if every single aspect of their parenting was somehow flawed.

I have to remind myself that my "flawed" parents raised six enormously successful children. They obviously did one or two things right.

I'm beginning to think it's not up to each generation to reinvent the wheel, but to maybe just find ways, with newly acquired knowledge, to tweak it a little so it runs more smoothly. Do we smoke and drink during pregnancy these days? Of course not. But our kids may find out someday that sports drinks and low-carb diets are harmful, and we'll all look back with a collective, "Oops!"

And, heck, maybe our kids will review our parenting and say, "Hey, you really shouldn't have made it so easy for us. You never made us work for anything, and you gave us everything we wanted simply because you could and because it was easier. When I have kids, I'm not going to be afraid to say 'no.'"

Or they might say to their children, "Boy, when I was young, our parents tried to talk us to death and reason things out all the time and protect us from every little disappointment! They made us play two sports all the time, even if it meant they were driving us all over creation and then waiting for us to be done! Can you believe it? You are so lucky I'm your parent and not your friend!" And their children will be sitting there thinking, "Yes, I get it. You had it worse."

Fortunately I know that someday they will get it, just like every generation before them — that they don't know everything and that their father and mother didn't do every single thing wrong. They will eventually understand that some of the stuff they went through was worthwhile and worth saving and worth passing on, that some of their childhood was actually pretty good, just like — well, when I was a kid.

—⁂—

MY YOUNGEST BROTHER RECENTLY ANNOUNCED his engagement, and asked if I had any advice for him, since my husband and I just celebrated our tenth anniversary.

I thought for a moment and said, "Yes. Keep dating."

There was a pause over the phone, and then he said, "Really? Are you sure? I thought that was one of those things, you know, that you give up when you get married...?"

I hung my head and sighed. Patience, Mag, I thought. He's a newbie.

"Not other people, you idiot," I said gently. "Keep dating each other. Have a date night, like every Friday, and go out together."

"Date my wife, huh?," he said. "OK. Right. Uh-huh. Do I have to, like, have her home by 10 p.m.? Hahaha...date my wife...good one!" He hung up chuckling.

I knew he didn't understand, and I knew that he wouldn't, truly, until he'd been married for awhile and maybe had a child or two. He simply wasn't at that point where romance and passion maybe don't come as easily as they once did. And I also know that even when we're at that point, understanding the concept isn't necessarily enough, either.

For example, I crawled into bed the other night at 10 p.m. The kids were asleep, finally, after the requisite stories, arguments over teeth-brushing, recaps of the day and glasses of water. The dog was in his crate. The laundry was folded and lunches made for the next morning. I was wearing my favorite old faded nightgown, and my pillow never felt so good. My eyelids started to flutter the second I lay down.

Then I felt a nudge.

I opened one eye and focused it on my husband, who was smiling and giving me his best come-hither look. I smiled back at this man I love and said the first thing that came to mind.

"You're kidding me, right?"

I just wasn't in the mood — for that, anyway. Apparently, however, I was in the mood for a little chat, because I spent the next 15 minutes listing the various reasons I was not in the other mood. They ranged from the cat puking on my shoe to the dog eating my fund-raiser order to the kids' chaotic practice schedules and my husband's barbaric need to get up before dawn.

"Honey," he asked, exasperated, "what can I do? Rub your back? Foot massage? What? What do you need?"

I thought about it, and finally said, "Empty the dishwasher. Make the coffee for the next morning. Have the kids in bed when I get home from teaching my night class. Take charge of deciding what's for dinner sometimes. Walk the dog without being asked. This kind of thing," I wrapped up, "is what turns me on."

"Roger that," he replied. "Um...tonight's probably a no-go then, huh?"

To answer his question, I turned over and went to sleep.

It's the truth. Traditional romance can get watered down a little once there are kids in the picture; who doesn't imagine the horror of a child walking in while mom and dad are *in flagrante delecto*? With light-sleeping children, the vision of years of therapy bills surrounds us each and every time my husband and I try to remember how we made them in the first place.

Sex and passion have to be worked on to be sustained. When the busyness of life takes over, it's easy to take the relationship for granted, to let the can't-wait-to-see-you-again feelings for each other fade. Throw menopause into the mix, with the hot flashes and night sweats, and the idea of passion goes the way of skinny jeans...with about as much relief.

Even I would have thought it amusing 10 years ago, the possibility that housework could someday be foreplay. So even though he thinks it's funny right now, I need to thank my brother for reminding me about a part of marriage that's become easy to forget. I need to thank him for making me think about my marriage at all.

And I need to tell a certain fella that I'm free for dinner on Friday night.

—❦—

ONE OF MY FAVORITE WRITERS has a unique way of dealing with her physical insecurities as she gets older. She's decided that instead of hating her sagging bottom and cottage-cheese thighs, she would treat them as lovable eccentric aunts along for the ride. It's how she is able to wear a bathing suit in public.

I may have to adopt her approach.

No, no, it's OK. You don't have to try and make me feel better. I'm a mature adult. I can see the writing on the wall, or in this case, the ripples on the rump. I don't have a 20-year-old body anymore. Well, actually, I do...twice.

And, no, all you fit and muscular forty-somethings out there, I know it isn't just an age thing. Don't go getting your spandex in a bunch. I know I could be in great shape, even at my age and after having given birth twice. I could exercise regularly and eat well just like you do...if it weren't so darn hard. (Sigh.)

So anyway, my daughter has been invited to her best friend's pool party at a local health club.

"Sounds fun," I said to the mom. "How'd you get them to close the club for you on a Saturday?"

"Oh, it's not closed," she said. "I've just reserved part of the pool at lunchtime."

So what you're saying, then, I didn't reply, is that I'll be wearing a bathing suit in a place in which I refuse to even appear in sweats, at the busiest time of day on the busiest day of the week. Lovely.

But I'll go, because it's my daughter's friend's birthday and my daughter loves to swim. And I'll get in the pool because as much as she loves to swim, she sinks like a stone. And I'll dig out my bathing suit and shoehorn myself into it, because that's what's expected of me. And I'll attempt to do all of this with a modicum of self-respect...or at least without crying.

And it's funny, in a way. As a youth I struggled with my body image because I *thought* I was too heavy or out of shape. As an over-40 mom, I struggle because I am.

It would have been so much easier to accept if the changes were gradual, but they were not. My breasts started reaching for my knees the day I got pregnant, and my butt — I'm not making this up — dropped last Thursday. Just like that, it was two inches lower. The bottom that used to jiggle when I jogged now wobbles when I walk.

And then we have the hair issue, with which I am beginning to take exception now that shaving season is back. (*What?* What do you mean, some women shave all year round? Who told you these lies, and why do you insist on spreading them?!)

Why is it, for instance, that the only thinning hair on my body is on my head? Is it a follicular conspiracy of some sort? Do they all get together and giggle and whisper things like, "Hey, I know! You guys on her head, fall out — and the rest of us on her face and legs and arms will grow more! Wouldn't that be funny?!"

I suppose I should at least be grateful that pale skin is

socially acceptable for the first time in my life; the other moms won't be clamoring over each other to sit next to me so they can feel tan. The multi-dimpled look, however, is evidently still taboo; one young mom has already started buddying up because she knows that next to my thighs, hers will look positively buff.

Is it an age thing? Possibly. Most of the moms of my daughter's little friends gave birth at a point in their lives when their bodies were still capable of springing back. Childbirth for me coincided with the natural migration south of most body parts, and while I wouldn't trade my experience for the world, I bet those body parts are hoping to God they don't scrape the ground when one of the kids jumps on my back.

The truth is, I've never felt comfortable in a bathing suit. I could have a supermodel's body (well, I *could* have, you know) and still be self-conscious walking around half naked. The good news about my age ("Hello, I'm menopause! Welcome!") is that I usually don't remember how self-conscious I am. Of course, that's also the bad news.

That said, I must go. The aunties and I must dress for a party.

—⚹—

"DO YOU SELL SAND"? I asked the cashier at the home store.

"What kind are you looking for?" she asked.

"The kind you put in a...oh, jeez, what's it called — the square plaything —" For the 14th time that day I couldn't think of the word I needed.

"Sandbox?" she asked, looking at me sympathetically. Good Lord, I thought. I just used the first half of the word and still couldn't think of it. She obviously had children and was over 40, or the sympathy look would have been more of a "lady, are you OK?" look. Believe me, I know the difference. I've gotten them both enough times lately.

I honestly don't know what's going on here. I mean, sure, I've done all the reading about pre-menopausal brain fog and the memory issues associated with aging, but it's all made to sound so benign, amusing even. Well, let me say this to the powers that be, whoever you are: I am not amused. My husband might be, but I am not.

I used to think it was funny, I'll admit. I'd joke about how some people forget their grocery lists, while I forget to go to the store. But we're beyond that sophomoric humor, my friends. I am now writing notes in the bathroom to remind me to look at a note in the bedroom which reminds me to add something to my grocery list in the kitchen.

It's like one of those strings people use to follow an unfamiliar path, or the ropes that are used in mountain climbing so that people can find the trail back down. My rope, sadly, is used to retain a thought.

Need more? I came out of the mall recently after having had lunch — LUNCH — not a four-hour shopping spree — lunch. And I couldn't remember where I parked. And it wasn't the cute, "Oh, silly me, I'm in the next row over," it was, "Oh my God, someone stole my car! Wait — what was in my car? Garbage? Who'd want to steal my garbage?" As I stood there mulling this over, a kindly young man approached and timidly asked, "Um, can I help you find your car?"

As though I were 90. And when I'm 90, maybe I will

graciously accept the offer. But I'm not 90. "No, you may not," I snapped. "I'm perfectly capable of finding my own car." And I did…30 minutes later.

At least that was a more or less private humiliation. The public ones are not as easy to sweep under the rug, assuming I'd even remember to get out the broom. These include the requisite forgotten appointments, birthdays and anniversaries. They also include the time I invited people to play golf, and then forgot to show up.

In that same vein, I invited my in-laws over for dinner on my golf league night. It's been on Monday nights for three months, and yet I called and said, "Want to come over for a cookout on Monday night?" I told my husband later that day and he reminded me that I actually golf on Monday nights. So that was nice. "Hi! Come on in! How are you doing?! Great! Gotta go! Have a good time! Bye!"

My kids think it's a riot, this memory issue, and have figured out how to turn it to their advantage. "Mom, don't you remember last time telling me I could have this toy the next time we came here?"

"Mom, I asked you if I could have a sleepover with 15 friends and you said yes. You just don't remember."

"Don't you remember that you said we could go to Disney World this summer?"

So I'm taking control. I bought some super-powered, "Scientifically proven!" herbal supplements that are supposed to go directly to the part of the brain that is misfiring and improve, specifically, short-term memory. There are studies that show

how this works. It's all very technical and medicinal-sounding. Unfortunately I have no idea if they work.

I can't remember to take them.

—⁓—

AUTUMN HAS ALWAYS BEEN ABOUT beginnings in my life. It's my season of rebirth, each and every year. I remember the fall 12 years ago when I adopted the first love of my life, a golden retriever named Decker. I was single, had no children, and had my dream career working from home as a writer.

Then I got married (in the fall) and had children (in the fall), and each autumn continued to breathe new life into me. I was fortunate enough to have the choice to stay home with my kids, and a new career was born. Days were spent changing diapers and feeding and potty training and harnessing tantrums and keeping nap schedules and walking the dog. Work was squeezed in when possible.

The fall that my son began preschool marked yet another beginning, the start of many years of dropping off and picking up every couple hours, three years for him and three for her, followed by half-day kindergarten for each. Days were spent in increments of three hours, doing what could be done in that time and getting the rest in — nap times, meals, errands, and work — the best I could. I often secretly wished for more time, careful not to wish away their childhoods.

Now it's fall again, and the kids are in school again. We have a new puppy to help fill the void left by my beloved Decker, and my days start out the same as they ever did. The husband gets up earlier than what should be legal, which wakes the puppy up even though he probably would have slept another two hours. He hops in the shower and I trudge downstairs, bleary, to let the dog out to do his business, which at this age he still assumes is done with an audience, rain or shine.

Shortly thereafter the boy gets up to his bird-call alarm and I trudge upstairs to start his shower because the faucet is so sensitive that one wrong hairpin turn will scald him. I then head back downstairs to feed the dog and cat and to get coffee. After the boy comes down, I wake up the girl and get her downstairs. Then I make the kids' breakfasts and hustle them back upstairs to get dressed and brush teeth. I make and pack their lunches and hunt for change for ice cream.

I assemble completed homework and miscellaneous paperwork for their folders, fill up their backpacks and zip them up. The girl's hair is brushed and appropriately clipped back, glasses are cleaned, sneakers tied. I go out to the bus stop and chat with the other moms after the bus pulls away. Eventually we all acknowledge we have to go; one of the moms' remaining at-home child is calling to her through the screen door, the other is going to work. I take my cup of coffee and head inside.

And I stand there.

It is completely silent. There is no radio playing, no television rambling in the background. The puppy's asleep on the kitchen floor. I take another drink of coffee and think, OK, now what do I do? I have some time, finally; for the first time in nine years, I have eight hours with no children. I'm at a complete loss as to what to do with myself.

I try to determine the problem, because certainly there are things I could be doing — nine years' worth of cleaning springs to mind. But I can't quite put my finger on it, for the umpteenth day in a row. I'm just...sad, somehow. Empty.

And guilty.

I feel guilty being alone, as if secret wishes through the years somehow created this void in my world. I feel as if I don't deserve this free time, this time to myself. My job is to take care of others, to do for others. I feel like I should be doing something for somebody, because for nine years, that's what I did, all day, every day. There was not one waking moment — nor many sleeping, for that matter — when taking care of those children was not on my mind on some level. I was their teacher, mentor, cook, housekeeper, entertainment, laundress, stylist, social secretary, chauffer.

Now, for all intents and purposes, I've been relieved of those duties. I chose to be a stay-at-home mother, a 16-hour-a-day job, and my hours just got cut in half. I'm not used to thinking anymore about things other than my children; I'm not used to thinking about me or my interests or about what I can do, maybe, for people besides my children. It seems somehow unnatural now.

It's autumn once again, and once again I have a puppy to train and my days free. But I'm not the same person I was back then, so things will be different. I may still feel weird for awhile, I know, and I think that's OK. But fall is for beginnings, and I know there's a new beginning out there for me somewhere. It just might be difficult to find at first.

After all, I'm a mother, and that's a tough act to follow.

—⁓—

Acknowledgments

I GRATEFULLY ACKNOWLEDGE the assistance of some very special people: Tina Schwab Grenis, whose editing is surpassed only by her friendship; my other T-girls, Tracey Prokop and Tammy DiDomenico, for their patience and attention to detail — both of which, it turned out, were very necessary; and Reid Sullivan, for her relentless encouragement and streamlining of my words. Thank you, as well, to Ralph, Renny and Sophie, the loves of my life, without whom I would have no desire to write...and nothing to write about.

—ᘐᘐ—